A SALE IS A LOVE AFFAIR

Seduce, Engage & Win Customers' Hearts

JACK VINCENT

Special thanks go to

Lisa Gerber for her strategic guidance, online and off.
BigLeapCreative.com

Barbara Schelling for her cover design and interior layout.
bschelling.com

Paul Pacitti for the portrait photo on the back cover.
flickr.com/photos/luzern-switzerland/

Esthy Barmettler for *the heart* painting on the front cover…
artividuell.ch

A Sale Is A Love Affair
Seduce, Engage & Win Customers' Hearts

ISBN-13: 978-1505564310
ISBN-10: 150556431X

"If you could only love enough,
you could be the most powerful person in the world."

— Emmet Fox

*"Being deeply loved gives you strength.
Loving deeply gives you courage."*
— Lao Tzu, Tao Te Ching

TABLE OF CONTENTS

1

WHEN SALLY MET HARRY

Sally met Harry at a networking event, and Harry made a great first impression.

"But don't they all?" Sally thought.

Sally was new in town. She had taken a job as Marketing Communications Manager for a major international firm, and her first two months on the job were manic.

She had hardly come up for air. She'd hardly had time to think about how non-existent her social life was, even though she was *feeling* it.

Perhaps it was her fear that the transition wasn't going to be easy that was keeping her in the office more than the actual workload was. Starting college in her late teens was a cinch compared to moving to the other side of the country in her mid-30's.

Deep inside, Sally knew she needed to get out there and start meeting people.

So she showed up at the networking event a little late… and everyone was already talking. Everyone was in their happy little circles, engaged in their comfortable conversations, giving the impression that newcomers need not apply.

Sally felt her heart rate pick up.

"Oh, shit!" she heard that little voice in her head say. "How do I break in?"

She bought some time by checking her coat. Then she wandered over to the bar and ordered a glass of Chardonnay. Then she turned around, with no more excuses.

She was alone, and the rest of the room was filled with happy, chatting people.

Harry spotted Sally and invited her into his group. He joked that she may not want to be spotted with such a motley group, "but I'll risk introducing you to everyone anyway."

Sally's guard dropped. There was something about Harry that, subconsciously, she quickly began to trust. Sure, he saved her from the depths of the lonely hearts' club. But he was easy... confident... charming.

He seemed to have the place wired, yet he didn't have an air of self-importance.

Harry introduced himself in a way that piqued curiosity but wasn't long-winded, and then he asked Sally just the right questions about herself... and he listened.

He really listened. He asked good questions, and he listened some more.

Here and there, he dropped in a related anecdote about himself, so it didn't feel like an interrogation. It didn't feel like he had anything to hide, but he was clearly interested in Sally while making her feel part of his group, too.

After about 10 minutes, Harry introduced another potential lonely heart into the group, a man. He and Sally started chatting, and then Harry said, "I'll leave you two. I'm going to mingle a little bit."

He gave another warm smile to Sally, and moved his way in to another group.

"Wow!" Sally heard that little voice say. "This could be just what I didn't even know I was looking for."

She discretely kept her eye on Harry as her new colleague chatted on about his job. She smiled politely, yet all the while she hoped Harry would circle back to her before the end of the evening.

Sure enough, as the crowd started to thin, Harry approached Sally. "I've been thinking about something you said earlier. Why don't we have coffee, near your office, Thursday afternoon?"

Sally smiled. "How about a glass of wine, in town, Thursday evening?"

Harry knew the perfect place, and the wine date went very well. The glass of wine turned into two, and the conversation was warm yet spontaneous, easy yet meaningful.

He listened intently as Sally talked about her life, her work and her reasons for taking this new job. At the right moments, he briefly showed her how they were aligned by mentioning little things about himself, before asking Sally more about herself, going one layer deeper each time.

He listened with his ears *and* eyes, Sally noticed. She couldn't believe she was telling Harry so much… *trusting* him so much.

When the bill came, Sally insisted on splitting it, despite Harry grabbing it first when the waiter set it between them.

"Our first fight," Harry said, and Sally laughed. The older couple next to them grinned, seemingly at how well Sally and Harry were getting along.

It was on the sidewalk in front of the wine bar where Sally made her feelings clear. She put her hand on Harry's elbow, and said, "I've got a really good feeling about this, Harry."

Then she dashed off to catch her train… out to the suburbs… to her husband and kids.

No, no. This was not the beginning of a romantic affair. This was the beginning of a sale.

Harry was selling to Sally. He had seduced her, engaged her, and soon he would be winning her heart.

Sally was falling in love with Harry, strictly in a business sense, of course.

Within a few weeks, Harry was winning the heart of Sally's parents and siblings, um, management and peers and, ultimately, he won a long-term, happily-ever-after-with-occasional-tough-love relationship.

A sale is a love affair.

2

SALES, LOVE & LIP SERVICE

This is about sales… and love… and how you can sell more by loving more.

So let's talk about sex… baby.

Let's talk about you… and me.

Let's talk about picking up women… and men… and customers.

Let's talk about kissing… and cuddling… and understanding.

Let's talk about connecting… on a level that's so deeply human that it's spiritual.

Let's talk about trust… and why it's the most important aspect of romantic relationships and business development.

You've got a ticket to ride… a ride that will go from sex, no drugs, to rock 'n roll… from spirituality to psychology… from pitching to seducing… from listening to engaging… from winning hearts and persuading minds to winning deals and keeping happy customers.

Throughout our ride, we'll see that *A Sale Is A Love Affair* is more than just a metaphor. We'll see that trust is the biggest component of a romantic relationship and a business deal.

Trust takes a long time to build and a moment to break. So, the first stop in our journey is self-love. Before you can build a trusting, enduring relationship with anyone – be it a lover or a customer – you have to work on yourself, to love yourself first – not in an egotistic, selfish way, but in a holistic, almost spiritual way.

Of course, before you can build a relationship, you need to *start* one. You have to stand out and get your love interest's or business interest's attention. You have to be compelling enough for prospective partners to want to go deeper with you. In essence, you have to attract. You have to seduce.

But seduction alone is for narcissists. After you've attracted someone, it's vital to engage them. The sale, the relationship, is not about you, in the singular, but about both of you, in the plural. Prospective partners are craving to not only know that you have the goods, but to also *feel* that you understand them… their needs… their problems… their hopes… their dreams. Understanding is at the heart of engagement.

Then you need to win their hearts. You need to gain commitment… not just to win the deal, but to sustain the relationship.

The behaviors of a great lover or, shall we say, a great romantic partner, are so similar to those of a great salesperson that it's my deepest conviction that they are the same!

The best salespeople in any industry are *loved* by their customers. Sure, they have good product knowledge, but they know that buying is an emotional process.

The best salespeople are either gifted or skilled at seducing, engaging and winning hearts and minds. They have self-love, but they put the needs of their customers first or, at very least, equal to their own. They love their customers and, thus, they earn their customers' love.

Are you paying lip service to improving your sales performance because you're doing some deals? Well, maybe you could be doing more deals. Maybe another salesperson in your same shoes would be doubling your volume.

Stop telling yourself you're a great lover just because you're, um, doing it! Maybe another lover would be bringing your partner to sexual nirvana and, oh, yeah, supporting your partner in a happy family life. How's your *Kama Sutra* these days?

Stop telling yourself you're a great salesperson just because you're doing some deals.

Are you giving... almost unconditionally?

Are you forgiving... with an open heart?

Are you apologizing... without using the word "but"?

Are you sparking interest with simple and compelling stuff... and then peeling the onion by listening... *actively* listening... at least as much as you expect to be listened to?

Are you asking good questions... questions that not only seek information, but also stimulate your partner to think deeply and share generously?

Are you mitigating conflict... and coming out of difficult conversations with deeper understanding and deeper commitment?

Is *win-win* more than just an expression you use, but part of your life operating system?

If so, you're probably doing better than I am. Really. I'm not challenging you to be perfect. I'm not perfect. I'm challenging you – and me – to be better... to be different.

I'm hoping to make the link between falling in love and winning business so resoundingly meaningful that the related skills stick and you use them every day.

So let's redeem this ticket to ride... to love more... and sell more.

SALES IS LIKE SEX.
EVERYONE THINKS THEY DO IT WELL.

In 2012, The Sales Congress Warsaw engaged me to be the keynote speaker for their annual conference. A month earlier, the conference's founding sponsor, Poland's largest sales trade publication, interviewed me for the May cover story.

The editor asked me, "What's the biggest challenge in getting salespeople to embrace sales training?"

"That's easy," I quipped. "Sales is like sex. Everyone thinks they do it well."

That little voice in my head whispered, "Oops, there goes the speaking engagement."

Then I heard the editor roar with laughter. "I love it!" she said. "Let's go deeper there."

No, she wasn't coming on to me. She wanted a good story, and the conversation took off.

And this is at the core of why I write this book. Dating, falling in love and sustaining romantic relationships are more than metaphors for prospecting, selling and customer retention.

If you've ever worked with dating coaches and marriage/relationship counselors (I have), and if you've *also* ever worked with marketing consultants and sales trainers (I am one), you'll see that much of the behavioral skills they preach are virtually the same.

Some salespeople show up at workshops and feel they know it all. Some even talk about best practices, but when you put them in a role-play or go out in the marketplace with them, they don't put the best practices to *use.*

You have sex and it feels good. "Wow! I'm doing great!" as you roll over and fall asleep.

You're in a relationship. "Wow! I'm doing great!" as you communicate in your habitual way without affirming that your partner might need a little more or even a little less.

You make a sale and it feels good. "Wow! I'm doing great!" as a different deal gets away, but, hey, you made a sale.

Many people find themselves in sales roles by happenstance. Whether in a tech startup that needs to win early customers, or as a wine writer who wishes to consult for upscale restaurants, all of a sudden they find themselves out in the marketplace selling. They have a few failures. Then a few successes cloud their ability to objectively assess their skills and their need to improve. "Wow! I'm doing great!"

Let's take Claudine, a market research expert. After crunching numbers and making meaning for a few years, she was made Deputy Director of a business unit and was soon out in the market making sales calls with her Director.

They had a few failures, and then a few successes, and Claudine's view was, "Wow! I'm doing great!"

The firm didn't think sales were that great, however, as it was actually losing more pitches than it was winning, and it really wasn't getting enough pitches to start with.

In the industry's growth years, it didn't seem critical. Nobody felt the pressure because the market was growing, so securing new business here and there was relatively easy.

Then the industry flattened. Losing too many pitches meant declining market share, which meant lower revenues and lower profits. So the firm instituted sales training for everyone who was client facing.

Claudine complained that she could better use her time at her desk... not cold-calling clients or working on new business development, just servicing what had already been sold.

So early on in the two-day sales workshop, she was quite clear that she knew all this stuff. In fact, "*Everybody* knows this stuff!"

Halfway through the first afternoon, it was Claudine's turn to be the sales-person in a role-play at her table, and the assignment was to use the tools discussed so far.

And. She. Flopped.

Not only did she run the worst role play of the day, she used none of the *stuff* that, "*Everybody* knows!"

In her table's de-brief, Claudine's peers gave her some pretty tough feed-back, so Deputy Claudine pulled rank and said, "Oh, come on. This is a waste of time. I'm going back to my desk!"

Her Director wasn't very impressed. Nor were her peers.

What was under the surface? It turned out that, since she had joined the firm, Claudine had brought in one deal, and that particular client was one from her previous employer.

Her perceived prowess for sales helped earn her the promotion to Deputy, but she really wasn't very good in sales at all.

Even before the workshop, much of the business unit believed that Claudine *didn't do sales well.* And by the end of the workshop, many were joking that she must be terrible in bed, too. Yes, even the women in the group!

But Claudine is not alone.

For every salesperson that believes that he doesn't need to learn any new skills, there are ten salespeople that learn new skills but don't adopt them. They forget or abandon these new skills the next time they get out in the marketplace.

That's one reason companies should not waste their money on a one-off workshop, but invest in a mid- to long-term sales improvement plan.

It's also the reason I write this book.

By creating parallels between prospecting, selling and servicing with dating, romance and relationships, salespeople more easily remember newly acquired sales tools and put them to use in their next targeting exercise or face-to-face engagement.

It's not about the training. It's about the performance that follows. It's about *embedding* best practices.

Just about everyone can relate to dating, relationships and love. Although some of us are too shy to talk about it with mere acquaintances, we almost always pay attention to these topics and take note.

Love and sales are two human activities that really do go hand-in-hand. To be happy and successful, both romantic love and complex sales are about winning hearts and minds. In the early stages, both involve standing out, attracting or, in a sense, seducing.

Both require connecting at a deeper stage in order to move forward with any meaning. We must fully engage our partners or prospects to live happily and successfully with them.

Then we must continue to win their hearts every day, lest the business be lost, and so might the love.

Some romanticists shriek that it's crass to equate the skills of *sales* with the behaviors of romantic partnerships. Fine.

But I simply have not met a high-performing entrepreneur or salesperson who disagrees.

So while the material in this book can be used by lovers to improve their dating and deepen their relationships, it's written for salespeople who want to continually improve, who want to *love more and sell more.*

Know-it-alls need not apply. The true master is an eternal student. Only those who keep learning are the true masters.

After all, sales is like sex... and some people actually do it well.

I WANT YOU TO LOVE ME

The concept of love in business is not new.

Servant leadership, for example, is essentially all about love. It's about leaders achieving outstanding results by serving their people, while enabling and empowering *them* to also share the love.

Branding, as another example, is about building an emotional, some say, almost spiritual, connection. *Nirvana* is achieved when a brand builds a connection that is beyond rational. Great brands go so deep that they connect with the customer's value system, their sense of identity.

In his book, *Lovemarks – The Future Beyond Brands*, Kevin Roberts, CEO of Saatchi & Saatchi, gives many examples of brands that have such an emotional connection with their customers that they are beloved brands, or Lovemarks. These brands have reached marketing's promised land. Consumers worship them.

Apple has achieved *love status* with its users. Not only do Apple users love the brand, they evangelize it. They spread the love.

Paradoxically, some consumers don't love Apple at all. In fact, some even *hate* Apple.

And Apple is just fine with it.

Much like not all women love the same type of man, and not all men love the same type of woman, so it goes that not all brands are loved by everybody.

But those brands that stand for something, those brands that stand *out*, those brands secure a more defined niche and retain customers longer.

They gain loyal, committed, trusting, *loving* customers. This love usually grows and grows if, and only if, these brands stay true to themselves as they go about seducing, engaging and winning the hearts of, excuse the pun, the apples of their eyes.

Arguably, the ultimate discipline for getting customers to fall in love with you is not leadership or branding. It's sales!

At any given company, global or otherwise, a relatively small number of marketing people will be working on making customers fall in love with the brands.

Yet on any given day, those same companies could have thousands of people on the ground, calling and visiting prospects and customers.

It's hard to argue that it doesn't get any more personal in business, on such an important scale, than face-to-face sales.

Whether you're selling pension funds to institutional investors or homes to young couples, it's personal.

Selling is deeply personal.

Because buying is deeply emotional.

Those young home-buyers are trying to view things rationally, as they seek the right investment while keeping their families safe and dry, and while living in a neighborhood they can enjoy and afford.

But they are also taking a big leap. Their hopes and aspirations are almost always mixed with fear, uncertainty and doubt.

The concept of risk is not just at the top of their minds. It's deep in their hearts.

They are not only thinking things as they move through their purchase, they are *feeling* things.

The same goes at the B2B level. That pension fund manager? She wants a suitably high return on investment. Her duty is to enable the employer to pay retired workers for decades to come. That's a burden that could keep her up at night, whether it's her duty to all those deserving families or her fear of losing her job!

Rationale is important, but emotion is paramount. These are the people we pitch to every day.

Dale Carnegie nailed this in his legendary book, *How To Win Friends and Influence People*. According to Carnegie, "When dealing with people, let us remember that we are not dealing with creatures of logic as much as we are dealing with creatures of emotion."

Calculated or not, risk is a perception that strikes deep at most people's emotions, and that definitely includes the emotions of buyers considering something new.

There is only *one* thing that fully mitigates risk, and that's trust.

Trust is achieved through addressing rational thoughts, as well as emotions and feelings.

If you want to get someone to fall in love with you, the driving factor will be trust.

Sure, you must attract them or be attractive to them.

Even attraction is trust, albeit primal. Attraction is instantaneous, yet it comes from our ingrained chemistry of what we feel will help us survive and thrive. We are instantaneously attracted to what we believe will deliver that – be it nice eyes and a curvaceous figure, a confident demeanor and a bad-boy attitude, or whatever floats our individual boat.

After attraction, for the relationship to go anywhere significant beyond that, your love interest will have to trust you to deliver on the expectations that you've created at each and every phase.

That expectation might be nothing more than a sizzling-hot, one-night stand without kissing and telling. It might be 'til death do us part – in which case, *good in bed* might make the list of criterion for some and *good with kids* might top the list for others. So the more long-term the business relationship that you're pitching, the more scrutiny and due diligence you can expect to receive, with certain key deal-breakers at the top.

Can she trust you to deliver in sickness and in health?

Hmmm. Weren't we talking about sales? How did we get into love?

Fasten your seatbelts. Every chapter will make *some* reference to both. Call it one big metaphor, or call it the human condition.

Can customers trust you to deliver on what you pitch?

Is it what they feel they need, or even *desire*?

Will they fall in love with you and stay in love?

Getting customers like me to fall in love with you is not an ignoble objective.

As a prospective customer facing you, the salesperson, I *know* that you want me to fall in love with you.

The problem is, when you wine me and dine me and sleep with me… will you call me in the morning?

Customers *know* that you want *them* to love *you*.

But what they *really* want… is for you to love *them*.

To get customers to fall in love with you, to profess their undying love to you 'til death do you part, you have to love them *so much* that *you* will *walk through the fire* for them.

Will this work every time? Of course not! But it will work *more often* with those customers with whom you have a good fit.

In any industry, the star salespeople who endure through the decades are not pick-up artists, although great salespeople are indeed very good at initiating new relationships.

These salespeople have either the talent or the skill to help their long-term customers grow and prosper, all the while growing and prospering themselves.

These salespeople are *loved* by their customers.

They interact like great lovers, romantic partners and spiritual soul mates.

They are confident, and that alone is an initial attractor to prospective buyers, much like confidence in a man is a turn-on to a woman. (Hang with me, ladies. There's stuff for you later!)

These star salespeople stand out early in their customer conversations by opening with simplicity. Attraction is an emotion, and emotions are triggered *only* with simplicity. Early on, complexity is a killer, in a sale and in a love affair.

Star salespeople don't try to be all things to all people with their product any more than a divorced father of college students should try to change his attitudes to become attractive to a thirty-something who wants to build a nest before the next snowflake falls.

They know that their products and offerings may not be right for all prospects. As self-confident lovers, they don't fall in love with someone who won't fall in love with *them*. They qualify their prospects and, depending on their findings, either respectfully discard them and move on quickly, or drill down more deeply by asking great questions, listening actively and showing genuine interest.

They don't propose solutions too early. That almost always kills trust. Sure, if it's a simple solution and a low-price tag, it may actually be appropriate to go for a one-night stand, to close in a first meeting. Quickies work for some sort of products, but rarely in a deal that will be long-term.

The broader the solution and the higher the price tag, the more star salespeople will drill down to truly understand their prospects' challenges, opportunities and needs. In doing so, they can build a common vision with their prospects… perhaps even with an idealistic dream of 'til death do us part!

Star salespeople don't let uncomfortable questions turn into relationship killers or marital strife. They make their points in a winning way, but before that, they handle objections in a way that sustains trust and fosters love. When they hear an objection, they are secure in seeing it not as a deal-breaker, but as a desire to move forward. They seize such opportunities for *strengthening* the relationship.

They negotiate not with a transactional approach and the one-dimensional desire to extract all they can from a deal, but rather in an integrative fashion that nourishes a healthy relationship after the deal is done, so that both parties prosper and grow after the contract is signed, and well after the honeymoon.

When problems arise, they consider the customer's needs and feelings at least as much as their own. Simply put, if their partner isn't happy, they aren't happy.

Star salespeople won't stay forever in a relationship that becomes toxic for whatever reason, but if it is a worthy partnership with trust and vision, they won't give up too soon, either.

If they do have to move on, they do their absolute best to maintain the best interests of their former client while maintaining their own integrity. Like a marital break-up in a tight community, the way you leave clients, or even respond to being fired, can make or break you in preserving the future of your marketplace.

Great selling manifests itself in tactical skills that, with time, become ingrained behaviors. But it starts with a mindset, a heart-set.

It's all about love. The more you give, the more you get.

Love more. Sell more.

AND SO IT BLOSSOMED

About three years before starting this book, I became a single man again.

With no tactical planning, I launched a new venture, which could better be defined as an *adventure*, and oh, what an adventure it was.

Objective: Find love.

Product: Me.

Marketplace: *Anything that walked* would be an exaggeration. Any woman that I considered interesting, unique, sexy, available and with a good heart would be more accurate.

Niche: *Niche?* It wasn't defined at all, and this is where the plot thickens. It turned out to be women above 35 and no more than my age. Oh, what I forgot to tell you about Product Me: I was 54, at the time. (I had conveniently forgotten to tell *myself* that!)

Strategy: Strategy? Like I said, I hardly had a tactical plan. Damn the torpedoes! Full-speed ahead!

Indeed, I was commencing anew on that timeless and universal activity of dating, seeking romance and, I am unabashed to admit, wanting sex.

Again, I was in my mid-50's. The last time I had asked a woman for a date, I was in my mid-30's. Not only had I changed, but so had the market's *standard operating procedures*. Email didn't even exist the last time I had dated, let alone *Facebook*!

It felt a bit like the scene in *Sleepless in Seattle*, when Jay (played by Rob Reiner) tells Sam (Tom Hanks) that it's a whole new dating scene out there.

Jay: "There's even *tiramisu!*"

Sam: "What's *tiramisu?*"

Jay: "You'll find out."

Sam: "Well, what is it?

Jay: "You'll see."

Sam: "Some woman is going to want me to do it to her, and I won't even know what it is."

Sleepless in Seattle was 1993. Here I was, back in the marketplace, in 2011.

It was exciting. It was scary. It was uncharted. One thing about leaving your comfort zone, you learn.

All the while, I was running my business of sales advisory and training, with the mission of helping *my clients* learn new skills and apply them.

What I never expected was that these two worlds, prospecting and dating, selling and loving, were about to merge... or collide.

Selling and loving had more similarities and parallels than I even dreamed of the day the idea hit me or, shall I say, I hit it. I walked straight in to the metaphor and, in doing so, I led the way, for 25 salespeople.

I was leading a two-day workshop for the Europe, Middle East and Africa sales team of a financial advisory firm. Their sales process was complex because their buyers' purchasing processes seemed, at least to them, complex... kind of like those in the dating world see the opposite sex.

With every exercise, the parallels between selling and loving weren't just *obvious* in my mind, they were *distracting*. Finally, I couldn't help myself.

Just before lunch on the workshop's first day, we were discussing *buyer signals* and what the salesperson should do when a buyer goes quiet.

The team agreed that sitting back and watching the sale lose momentum, and tolerating uncertainty for any length of time, was far worse than taking the risk of possibly discomforting the buyer with probing questions.

So out came the flip-chart, where we listed different types of incisive questions that, the participants agreed, were within the salesperson's full right – that were within the salesperson's *duty*, in fact – to ask.

One sales exec put on his game face, mocking a client interaction. "I'm sensing some resistance on your side, Joe. Are there any concerns that I should know about?"

The team looked at me for affirmation.

Now my mom thinks I should have gone to drama school to be an actor, as I often tell stories by putting on little skits or, as she calls them, one-act plays. And off I went.

"It's a bit like love, don't you think? Like a husband and wife who aren't

25

talking to each other until one of them breaks the ice."

I put my hand on my hip and played the part of the wife. "You ain't talkin' to me, baby. What's the matter? We gotta' get to the bottom of this. So tell me straight, baby. What's botherin' you?"

It got a good laugh, but it didn't stop there.

Humor works in training, because it makes the material memorable – even more so when the participants begin contributing to the humor.

This turned out not to be just humor. It became a serious analogy that we kept coming back to throughout the remainder of the workshop.

For the next day-and-a-half, that joke morphed into our simile, our metaphor, our unexpected link between sales skills and that other deeply human behavior called love.

The metaphor created a hot link into the minds of the participants. It helped embed specific sales tools into the participants' memories... *and into their active skill set.*

Romance, relationships and dating became our call back joke for the rest of the session. And it *worked*!

Probing questions was just the start. The parallel went as far as closing the deal and sleeping with someone for the first time.

"I believe we've addressed all your concerns, Joe. How do you suggest we move forward?"

One of the lady participants was probably the salesperson who loved the sales-love metaphor more than anyone.

Her mischievous grin broke out again, as she quipped, "I'm a bit more straight forward. I usually say, 'Thanks for dinner, honey. Now, are we going back to your place?'"

It was beyond memorable for the participants. It helped them put the new tools into their active skill sets, and that is a facilitator's dream. Again, it's not about the training. It's about the performance that follows.

Since those sessions a few years ago, I haven't been able to get the metaphor out of my head.

> *The parallels between "successfully" finding a romantic partner and "successfully" selling to a new customer are crystal clear.*

I've discussed these parallels with business professionals, clients, colleagues and with very close friends of both genders and sexual orientation.

The naysayers say something like, "Oh, that's just crass. I don't want some guy selling his love to me!"

"Imagine a woman who's going to use sales skills on me. Come on, dude, I'm a bit more intelligent than that, thank you."

But the fact is, these naysayers tend to be people who have never been on the front line of sales.

Those who have sold, those who have led organizations that sell every day, often say, "Wow! It's actually so obvious."

A CEO who had been referred to me by a mutual colleague, said in our first meeting, "I've always seen this parallel, sales and love. In fact, you and I are on a blind date, don't you think? A referral is a blind date."

The metaphors are endless, and that's my biggest challenge in writing this book. Just when I think I've completed the book, another metaphor steps in my path.

I admit. It's become my obsession. A sale is a love affair.

6

IT CUTS BOTH WAYS

The good news is that this book is not about using sales tools in romantic relationships.

The bad news is that it could be.

Again, some people will vehemently disagree with the concept that the tactical tools of great salespeople are the very inter-personal tools that mere mortals should use when pursuing dates, securing a committed partner and sustaining a healthy relationship.

How crass!

To some people, yes. To others, no.

And here is where I challenge those who think it's crass.

Pick up a good book on sales training, or participate in a good sales training workshop. Then pick up a good book on dating and relationships, or sit down with a dating coach or marriage/relationship counselor.

So many of the soft skills are the same!

One's view of this is directly related to one's view of the discipline of sales and of salespeople generally.

Almost universally, those who have a positive view of the sales discipline also have a positive view toward the concept of sales skills being useful in a romantic relationship.

Those people who have a negative view of the sales discipline, conversely, have a negative view of this.

These naysayers believe that successful salespeople are pushy and only seek selfish goals, and that the successful people out on the dating scene are selfish pick-up artists.

Both of the above statements may have a degree of truth to them, but that does not mean they are entirely true, either. It does not mean that there is a full and absolute correlation between them.

So, to debunk this myth that tactical sales tools have no place in pursuing and sustaining romantic relationships, let's first start by debunking the myth that the discipline of sales generally – and salespeople specifically – are bad.

Sure, bad salespeople often use tactics that are slick, slimy and selfish.

But that is exactly what *great* salespeople *don't* do.

Again, great salespeople are loved by their customers and one does not attain the status of greatness today through manipulation.

To reiterate for the sake of this point, great salespeople have the tools to spark initial interest. They know how to paint a vision of a great future.

They then ask good questions… and listen. They diagnose before they prescribe. They build solutions not just *for* the customer, but *with* the customer. They propose only when they observe – and *feel* – that the customer is ready.

They negotiate in a win-win spirit, because they know that the future of the relationship is more important than the deal itself. They put the interest of their customer at the same level as the interests of their own company.

Great salespeople truly believe in partnership.

Who wouldn't want a romantic partner with those same interpersonal skills? Who wouldn't want a romantic partner that can be loved... and trusted?

Take a look at much of the material written in the mainstream press today, from business to romantic relationships, from *Fast Company* to *Psychology Today*.

These publications address everything from sparking interest in a prospect and potential partner, to qualifying leads and determining if "he's really Mr. Right," to resolving conflict and keeping the relationship happy and healthy.

To take it further to the point that it hurts, just look at all the people that are failing miserably in their dating and romantic relationships.

Are they failing because they're horrible people, ugly people, perverts and kidnappers?

Or is there a chance, a mere chance, that they repeatedly hook up with the wrong partners?

Is there a chance that they don't spark interest quickly and effectively?

Is there a chance that they talk too much about themselves?

Is there a chance that they don't ask their love interest enough questions and, when they do, they listen only for a nano-second before flipping the conversation back to themselves?

Is there a chance that they try to close the deal too aggressively, and don't let their love interest share the power in the decision?

Is there a chance that they breach the trust of their partner by not handling conflict or objections in a way that wins the point while not damaging the trust?

Is there a chance that they don't *do and say* the little but important things in relationships that build and sustain trust?

Some of the nicest people in the world do and say things that hurt their chances during the sale… oops, I meant, during the first date.

So while your love life may be thriving, and I truly hope it is, many people's love lives are just adequate at best. Many more are just plain stuck in the muck. Their love lives suck, and I'm not happy about reporting that.

Is there a chance that the most important concept in sales, building trust, is also the most important concept in finding romance and building strong relationships?

Is there a chance that all those people who are desperately yet unsuccessfully trying to meet their romantic partner – or who are failing at building meaningful relationships once they do get started – is there a chance that they are, um, poorly executing the tactics?

Is there a chance that if they incorporated the *soft* skills of great salespeople, they would be more successful in romance, in love?

Is there a chance that lovers can benefit from using the tools of salespeople who are loved by their customers?

Go ahead. Call it crass to use sales tools to find romance and to foster relationships. Hopefully you're already happy in a long-term relationship, or you already have whatever you want.

But if you're not, the choice is yours. Can you learn *something* from great salespeople? Can you learn maybe just *one* little skill from those business development types who are *loved* by their customers?

For decades, advertising thought leaders have written that the best brands create emotional connections.

Why is it that *love and branding* is guru-esque, while *love and selling* is crass?

It's my conviction that it's not!

The best salespeople *interact* in a way that shows love for their customers. In turn, their customers love them.

The happiest romantic partners are either naturals at using highly effective interpersonal skills or have learned them in self-help books, through trial and error, at leadership retreats... or in sales workshops.

Ah yes, this book is for all those out there selling. It's about selling more by loving more.

It isn't for all those out there romancing. It isn't about loving more by selling more... unless you want it to be.

SALESPEOPLE ARE FROM MARS. CUSTOMERS ARE FROM VENUS.

"Women need a reason to have sex. Men just need a place."

The above quote has been cited to more than one person, from French philosophers to Dr. Phil, and most notably in pop culture to comedian Billy Crystal.

Men and women *are* fundamentally different and, for this reason, much of this book will draw on this human dynamic.

Call me sexist, but, really, I'm not alone.

John Gray's landmark book, *Men Are From Mars, Women Are From Venus,* could well have described the respective relationship between salespeople and customers.

For starters, salespeople are typically pretty simple. They want to sell.

Customers want to buy, sometimes, not all the time, if everything is up to snuff, if they have a reason, if, if, if. Indeed, buying is a complex process.

In a B2B environment, the first level of customer complexity is multiple decision-makers and influencers. Consensus building and persuasion is pretty complex in itself.

The other B2B complexity is organizational risk. If a manager drives through a purchase and something goes wrong, the manager could lose credibility... and even her job.

Even in a B2C environment, consumers take a risk whenever they purchase something for the first-time or for the long-term. The higher the price tag, the greater the risk. The greater the risk, the more analysis and rational thinking is required... and the more emotional the purchasing process becomes.

This is one of the most overlooked areas of novice salespeople. Their customers are not only going through rational processes when they buy, they are going through emotional ones.

Some will call it sexist to equate women with emotion and complexity.

Let me take a stand right here and now! Ladies, you yourselves say this all the time. So attack this male writer if you will, but reflect on your own words, thoughts, and, um, emotions.

I exaggerate to simplify, but while we boys are out shooting pool, watching football and shallowly talking about chicks, you girls are having in-depth conversations. You're going deeper... and that is wonderful!

"Eine Frau hat sieben Siegeln," goes an old German saying. "A woman has seven seals."

Seals, in this case, refers to the wax closure that used to be put on confidential envelopes containing important letters. After a letter was inserted into the envelope, the envelope would be sealed by melting wax on the closure, and often marked with an identification seal.

That a woman has seven seals on her envelope means that women are almost impossible to understand.

Some women even say, "We don't even understand ourselves." This male writer is not criticizing but, rather, celebrating this. How humanly breathtaking it is, as a man, to hear a woman say, "Don't try to understand me. Just love me."

Ron Louis and David Copeland make a prolific point in their book, *How To Succeed With Women*, which really is not about how to become a pick-up artist, but, yes, how to get dates *and* how to have *successful* relationships.

Louis and Copeland say a woman will have a thousand reasons not to have sex with a man… until they *do*. Then they'll have a thousand reasons to justify that they did the right thing.

Again, this very much reflects buyer behavior. Let's say that a salesperson calls on a prospect in a medium to large organization. *Prospect* is typically one person or, at most, a few. But for the moment, let's say one person in the organization is motivated to buy a given product or service, and is motivated to choose this salesperson, his product and the organization behind him.

If the prospect assumes the responsibility to manage the internal culture of her organization to make your deal happen, this prospect is often called a *champion*.

Salespeople often rely on a champion within an organization to *champion* through a deal.

As she *champions* the deal internally, she will normally have to persuade a fair number of resistors. Some of these resistors are paid to do this. They're paid to resist new vendors. Be they senior managers or procurement departments, their role is to call for due diligence before any deal is done.

Other resistors will be situational. These can be managers who will work closely with the vendor once selected, staff who believe they may have a better way than yours or a better vendor than you, or those who simply believe the deal shouldn't be done at all.

Customers have a thousand reasons not to go to bed with just anybody, including you. How complex!

The salesperson on the other hand, just wants to get the deal done... unless, of course, he's qualified the prospect and believes that doing a deal will be too expensive, too time-consuming or, um, too high-maintenance.

But if the qualification passes the first test, keep it simple, damn the torpedoes and get the deal done. How simple!

John Gray himself outlines a behavior in *Men Are From Mars, Women Are From Venus* that is of striking importance in the man-woman relationship, that also applies in the seller-buyer relationship.

Often a man offers a solution to a problem that his woman brings up, only to find that the woman is not immediately interested in solving the problem. She merely wants to *talk* about it... to be *listened* to.

"The most frequent complaints women have about men is that men don't listen," Gray writes.

I must hold up my hand and admit, I didn't read Gray's book until recently... and mostly out of research for this book. When I came across the above, about listening and offering solutions, my jaw dropped.

As a man, I felt condemned. As a sales trainer, I felt validated.

For over a decade now, as a sales trainer, I have been preaching, "The most underrated sales tool is listening." Listening is the most important – and most overlooked – behavioral tool in persuasion and in selling.

Enough about specific sales tools per se for now. This is about human behavior, mindset... and heart-set. Let's not get hung up on the guy-and-chick thing. Let's just focus on human behavior.

Customers are complex. Salespeople are simple.

Ergo, much of this book will make the parallel of men pursuing women with salespeople pursuing customers.

I say "much of this book," not "all of this book."

This should not be taken in an absolute way. As a buyer can use listening tactics in handling a negotiation, so can a woman use seduction tactics in advancing a relationship. Perhaps I'm hedging here, in which case, so did John Gray.

Even Gray writes, "I make many generalizations about men and women in this book. Probably you will find some truer than others. After all, we are all unique individuals with unique experiences.

"Sometimes in my seminars, couples and individuals will share that they relate to the examples of men and women but in an opposite way. The man relates to my descriptions of women and the woman relates to my descriptions of men. I call this role reversal.

"If you discover you are experiencing role reversal, I want to assure you that everything is all right. I suggest that when you do not relate to something in this book, either ignore it (moving on to something you do relate to) or look deeper inside yourself. Many men have denied some of their masculine attributes in order to become more loving and nurturing.

Likewise many women have denied some of their feminine attributes in order to earn a living in a work force that rewards masculine attributes.

"If this is the case, then by applying the suggestions, strategies, and techniques in this book, you not only will create more passion in your relationships but also will increasingly balance your masculine and feminine characteristics."

Thank you, Mr. Gray.

As it is in love, it is in sales.

Customers need a reason to do a deal. Salespeople just need a place.

LOVE IS A SURVIVAL INSTINCT. SALES IS A SURVIVAL ACTIVITY.

"Love is the highest power." After all, we read stuff like that everyday on Facebook. It must be true. (Still with me?)

"Love is an animalistic, primal instinct." Bet you don't find *that* much on The Book of Face.

I like to see myself as a spiritual guy, and yet, some of my deepest spiritual beliefs are so primal that they're barbarian. There is no conflict, no gap, here. Science and spirituality are compatible!

So here goes. Love is such a fundamental part of our genetic makeup that it, at once, transcends our highest spiritual callings, while it also lies at the bottom of *Maslow's Hierarchy of Needs*.

That's why love is Yin Yang.

Love is the highest power.

Love is a survival instinct.

"You don't understand love," say some of the religious, not to mention the spiritual. "Love is not at the base of Maslow. Sex and reproduction are."

That actually makes the point. Love transcends it all. Love is at once spiritual nirvana, the Holy Grail. Love is also what drives us not only to procreate, but to care for our families, our loved ones, our tribes.

"*Watch out for the car!*" a mother shouts at her son.

Why? Because she loves him and, in that way, she contributes to his survival.

Love is indeed a higher power, but it is *also* a survival instinct.

And sales is a survival activity.

Without sales, we die.

Without sales, there is no commercial activity. Without commercial activity, there is no business activity. Without business, there is no work. Without work, there is no money. Without money, we don't survive – at least those of us who live on the grid who are probably reading this book.

Without sales, nobody survives.

In order for anyone to sit at a desk, someone has had to sell somebody something on their organization's behalf. At a minimum, the person sitting at the desk has had to sell *themselves* at a job interview.

Even people far removed from the sales and marketing department would not be producing something, cooking something, cleaning something, delivering something, managing something, teaching something… if someone hadn't *sold* something.

That university professor? The university either needs to secure student tuition or get funding from the government.

Even governments, in spite of carrying a big stick, have to sell the need to pay taxes.

Sales is at the bottom of any *Commercial Hierarchy of Needs*. Without a sale, nobody survives.

At the same time, sales is at the top of the *Operational Hierarchy of Needs*. With sales, we thrive.

Look at any successful company, brand or product. Look at any successful consultant. Look at any successful start-up. The single-most measurable component of success is sales.

Sales is what makes you king of the jungle.

Sales is what makes you the darling of Wall Street.

Sales transcends any organization's highest calling.

Sales is what enables you to reach nirvana and to share it.

Sales is the highest power.

Love is the highest power.

Love is a survival instinct.

Sales is a survival activity.

Love. Sales. Survival. Nirvana.

Yin Yang defined.

9

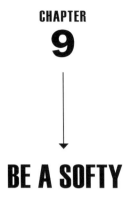

BE A SOFTY

I was once finalizing an agreement with the CMO of a mid-size venture capital firm, whose business development people were mostly investment managers that had been moved into sales roles.

As CEOs can interrupt anyone's meeting, the firm's CEO walked unannounced into the meeting room and said, "Hi Jack. I have one question for you. You don't know venture capital. Why should we hire you?"

"You're right," I said. "I don't know venture capital. You do."

The CEO was surprised. I think he wanted me to squirm and make the case that I was learning, and that I would commit to learning more.

"*You* know venture capital," I continued. "That's not why you're hiring me."

"Help me out a bit more," he said.

"Your people have all the hard skills of venture capital, risk, return and all that stuff. They're excellent at those hard skills. But they're underperforming at the soft skills."

"Oh no. Don't get all soft on me," he laughed.

"Sales!" I said. "Your salespeople open the door to a new prospect, and they go in with an investment manager, and between the two of them, they do 80 per cent of the talking. Perhaps I'm over-simplifying, but they present, and then they take questions."

He looked at me with skepticism.

So, I asked him, "When you leave a first meeting with a new prospect and you reflect back on the meeting, who did most of the talking? You, or the prospect?"

He admitted that almost always, he and his people do significantly more talking than the client does. With further probing, he admitted his team typically did much more than 50 per cent of the talking.

"But that's what clients in our industry want," he insisted. "They call us in so that they can get to know us and our investment opportunities."

"Of course they want to get to know you," I replied. "But even though they don't say it, even though they themselves might not even *know* it, what they *really* want is for you to get to know *them*.

"They getting to know you," I continued, "is no reason to hire you, to invest with you, to buy from you. What they need is to *trust* you. Would you trust a doctor who only pitched his services and didn't ask you questions and listen? Of course, investors want to know that your team is competent at the hard skills of investing.

"But to really trust you," I continued, "they need to feel that you've done the *soft* things of understanding *them*. You brag about this on your website, that you understand your clients. You need to *show* it when you're face-to-face with *prospective* clients. You need to *do* it, and ask them the right questions. You need to listen to them, as part of your skill set."

"This is funny," the CEO said, now involving the CMO in the conversation. "Just this morning in the kitchen area, I overheard one of our lawyers say she met a guy last night at an expat event. At first she liked him, but he didn't stop talking about himself, and that really turned her off. So when he asked her for her number, she didn't give it to him."

"Was it one of your salespeople?" I poked.

He laughed. "No wonder they're all single."

"A sale is a love affair, George. The soft skills are critical."

"A minute ago, you said our prospects need to trust us, and I agree. Now you're saying they need to fall in love with us."

"What's the difference?" I asked.

The CEO looked at the CMO and said, "Keep this guy around. We don't need a sales coach. We need a love coach."

10

LOVE, TRUST & ACCEPTANCE

Robert Plutchik's Theory of Emotion is among the most influential works for classifying emotions, as well as for outlining human responses when emotions are triggered.

Plutchik, a Psychology PhD from Columbia University and Professor Emeritus at Albert Einstein College of Medicine, proposed that humans have eight primary emotions: anger, fear, sadness, disgust, surprise, anticipation, trust and joy.

These emotions are biologically primitive, according to Plutchik. Each is a trigger of behavior with high survival value, such as the way fear triggers a fight-or-flight response.

Plutchik stated that even primary emotions are hypothetical constructs or idealized states. Each emotion can trigger varying degrees of intensity or levels of arousal within any individual. Yet the evidence is clear that there is a link between emotional triggers and emotional responses.

Right next to the emotion of *trust* on Plutchik's Wheel of Emotion is the quality of love and the behavior of acceptance.

Clearly, trust is a component of love. We trust that our partner will do certain things that attracted us into the relationship in the first place. Perhaps it was seduction that attracted us initially, but moving forward, other qualities deepen the relationship and we develop love for someone that we trust will behave in certain ways.

Love influences trust.

Trust is the biggest component of a sale.

One of the fundamentals in selling today is that salespeople should act in a way that moves them away from the traditional *salesperson* image. Many companies have renamed the sales discipline, in fact, to *business development*, and even *customer relationship*, believing that the title *salesperson* might scare away clients and that these newer titles are more trustworthy.

To be perceived as a mere *vendor* has become a competitive disadvantage. Today, the most successful salespeople are seen by their clients as *trusted advisors*.

Trust mitigates risk.

Whenever you ask someone to buy something from you for the first time, you're asking them to take a risk.

Risk triggers emotions such as fear, which generates thoughts that lead to uncertainty. While sales negotiations often come down to pricing, getting buyers to the negotiation table in the first place is a long process. This process usually involves, in some shape or form, attraction, seduction, understanding, aligned vision, compatibility, character, competence, solution-building.

Then, and only then, can *acceptance* be achieved in the form of an agreement, in the form of a sale.

Interestingly, on Plutchik's Wheel, *acceptance* is right between trust and love.

If your romantic partner is going to accept your proposal to move in together or get married, isn't trust a fundamental driver in your decision to accept?

If your client is going to accept your proposal to invest in your agency's branding proposal, isn't trust a fundamental driver?

Trust building is paramount to successful loving... and successful selling.

The Bucket of Trust is a great analogy. The act of trust building is like filling a bucket with water, one drop at a time. It takes a long time to fill this bucket, but it takes only a minute to empty it, to kick it over with one simple breach of trust.

After *The Bucket of Trust* is emptied by a breach, somehow the next time you try to fill it, the drops come more slowly, if at all.

It's hard work, building trust, and the bad news is that it can be breached in a moment.

Whether you're seducing, engaging or winning hearts, your customers will, consciously or unconsciously, be continually assessing their risk and trust factors. Only then will they reject or accept.

Trust is your most treasured currency... in sales and in love.

11

THE HEART FEEDS ITSELF FIRST

Nearly every journey into spirituality touches upon, perhaps even *begins* with, the concept of self-love.

If the S-word, spirituality, scares you, then substitute the P-word, psychology. So much of the spiritual work being done today, by gurus and seekers alike, overlaps with psychology.

Spiritually, self-love is not ego. It is not putting your self-serving needs above those of others. That's selfishness, and that's based on fear and scarcity.

True self-love is about hope and abundance. Those with healthy self-love are better partners in almost any relationship, be it friendship, love or business.

After returning from a week-long spiritual retreat, a friend posted on Facebook, "The heart feeds itself first."

The heart not only distributes blood to the rest of the body and other organs. The heart *needs* blood. The heart is an organ, not to mention, a hard-working muscle, at that.

If the heart feeds itself first, is the heart being selfish? The brain doesn't think so. The muscles don't think so. The other organs don't think so.

If the heart didn't take its biologically-designed commission upfront, if it had to wait 30 days for the invoice to get paid, the other organs would also be forced to stop taking care of business. No thinking. No feeling. No movement. No sex. No survival of the organism, and no survival of the species.

A healthy, well-fed heart is simply a better partner for the entire organism.

In romance, as in business, strong, healthy individuals make strong, healthy partners. So let's start with romance first.

Some of the most distressed relationships today are those in which one partner (or both) lacks a healthy balance of self-love. Conversely, the healthiest relationships are those consisting of two strong partners, who each value themselves as much as they value the other.

Tara Parker-Hope wrote in *The New York Times*, in December, 2010, *The Happy Marriage Is The 'Me' Marriage*. While this concept would have ruffled the feathers of your great grandmother, in today's world, it's reality.

Parker-Hope quotes Monmouth University professor, Gary Lewandowski. "If you're seeking self-growth and obtain it from your partner, then that puts your partner in a pretty important position. And being able to help your partner's position would be pretty pleasing to yourself."

Lewandowski goes on to say, "While the notion of self-expansion may sound inherently self-serving, it can lead to stronger, more sustainable relationships."

So, not only is it ok to seek self-fulfillment from our relationships, it's necessary. The heart feeds itself first!

Love yourself. It's ok. You're good. You're whole.

I've worked with startup entrepreneurs who love their product and love their mission to change the world, but they get a pang of discomfort about selling. When they think of selling, they feel like money mongers. Yet they need money in order to achieve their mission.

I've had coffee with many friends of all ages who want to find romance, but they feel like perverts. Going out with the intention to meet someone of the opposite sex makes them feel uncomfortable with *themselves*.

As a man or woman longing for a romantic partner, you are not a pervert. Sure, sex is one of your wants. That, in itself, is not abnormal. That is a primal need, and it is human. You are not a misfit. You are a human being seeking a deep connection.

Know that you can help the right lady of your life have a meaningful life, as she can help yours. Know that you can bring happiness to the right man in your life, as he can bring happiness to you.

And so it is in business partnerships. As a salesperson, an independent consultant or the entrepreneur of a startup, it's up to you to forge new relationships and to keep them strong.

Cultivate self-love. Be absolutely confident that you can add value to your customers... specifically those customers that can see your value-add. There are toxic customers out there just like there are toxic romantic partners.

You are not a sales dog. You are a professional seeking partnership where fair value is exchanged. With that comes mutual respect, understanding and communication.

As it is perfectly ok to desire love, it is perfectly ok to monetize your startup, to drive the top line for a worthy business mission.

You need to sell. And you need to love. You're good. You're whole. Love yourself. Respect yourself. Feed yourself first, emotionally and spiritually, and you will be a great candidate for a great partner, in business and in romance.

Close your eyes. Take a deep breath. Exhale slowly, and tell yourself you're all right.

"I'm good. I'm whole. I love me."

12

IF YOU WANT THEM TO BELIEVE IT, YOU GOTTA' LOVE IT

The central theme of this book, the mantra, if you will, is that in order to win new business and keep existing business, you need to be truly customer-focused and *love your customer*.

But that should not overshadow how important it is to love your *stuff*, too. It's consistent with self-love.

The only way to get customers to *believe* your stuff is for you to *love* it first. The word *passion* might be over-used today, but the concept is central to selling: when you infinitely believe in your product, *passion* just emanates from you.

When you're passionate about your *product*, you'll be passionate about bringing it to the *marketplace*, to those *customers that you love*.

Passion is contagious. Passion alone attracts, seduces and engages. This *love of your stuff* invariably sparks a virtuous cycle. It sets hearts on fire!

In *Bono On Bono*, the iconic U2 lead singer recalls the day the band left the studio after recording its sixth album, *Rattle and Hum*.

U2's previous album, *The Joshua Tree*, had been a blockbuster. Songs like *With Or Without You* and *I Still Haven't Found What I'm Looking For* had topped the charts.

While recording *The Joshua Tree*, the band wasn't convinced this would be the case. They felt they had set the studio on fire, but they also felt that the material might be *too far out there* for the masses, that the public would not dig their mojo. They actually had felt this in their first four albums before that, as well.

Each time, they were wrong. The public loved U2's stuff, and the band rocketed from one success to another into the rock 'n roll stratosphere.

Then came *Rattle and Hum*.

The music executives wanted to be part of this success, and the planning for *Rattle and Hum* began to sound like boardroom drivel of market trends, target audiences and focus groups.

The band went along with the business guys… and lost sight of their passion.

So here they were, leaving the studio after *Rattle and Hum*. Bono and lead guitarist, Edge, looked at each other and, for the first time, said, "Everyone's going to love this one!"

And. It. Flopped.

My, how insightful they *weren't*.

My, how *passionate* they weren't.

Passion rules!

Some of the most successful products don't hold water in many boardrooms. Consensus is often the nemesis of innovation and success, and that's where many entrepreneurs get it right. They're not confined by the boardroom. They're not developing their stuff while hoping for the approval of corporate types.

As *Owner Media Group* CEO, Chris Brogan, posted on Facebook one morning, "On paper, pretty much anything that's amazing and/or new doesn't work. Beastie Boys, for instance."

Conversely, what often looks logical on paper doesn't fly in the marketplace. It doesn't resonate in customers' hearts.

It's all about love.

If you're bringing something to the marketplace that you don't believe in, that you don't truly love, then you just won't reach your full potential.

So, yes, when you engage with your customers, love them. But don't forget that the starting point is loving yourself... and loving your product.

If you don't love it, fewer prospects will believe it, and they won't buy it!

U2 learned a hard lesson in 1988... but they indeed learned it.

Three years later, when they went into the studio to cut Album 7, *Achtung Baby*, they basically told the music executives to take their focus groups and buzz off.

The band had been advised that the song, *One*, could offend mainstream listeners, particularly Catholics.

Bono, himself, is a devout Catholic, and this warning only made him believe in his lyrics, his *stuff*, even more.

Have you come here for forgiveness?
Have you come to raise the dead?
Have you come here to play Jesus
to the lepers in your head?

When U2 finished recording *Achtung Baby* and left the studio, Bono and Edge looked at each other and laughed at themselves... at how crazy they were... and at how much they loved the material.

And *Achtung Baby* went through the roof in sales and reviews. *One* topped the charts. It won over critics, and it truly touched the hearts of millions of spiritual seekers and music lovers alike.

One is felt by many to be prophecy, and I personally have never heard of prophets checking their ideas with focus groups. Prophets are the first ones to love their stuff.

Great selling requires customer-focus, no doubt. But it also requires deep belief in your product, in your content, in yourself.

It's religious. It's spiritual. It's rock 'n roll.

I know. It's only rock 'n roll, but I like it, love it, yes... I do.

↓

TO THINE OWNSELF BE TRUE

Shakespeare was on to something.

If he were alive today, he'd be highly sought after by conference organizers and marketing directors alike, not to mention the self-help world of living your dream.

"To thine own self be true" speaks to your USP, your unique selling point, your point of differentiation, your competitive advantage. It also speaks to strong relationships that begin with knowing your authentic self.

David Deida is indeed alive today, and he writes fascinating stuff about masculinity and spirituality, and sex and relationships. He focuses on how to be whole with yourself, and how to live happily in a partnership.

In his 2004 book, *The Way of The Superior Man – A Spiritual Guide to Mastering the Challenges of Women, Work and Sexual Desire*, Deida writes that your mission is important. Your purpose in life is your gift. Your higher calling is key to your character.

Your relationship should support that, not get in the way of that. If it does get in the way of your life mission, you will regret it later.

Being called off from your mission at the insistence of your loved one will negatively impact that love and, ultimately, the relationship will become toxic.

Moreover, it will thwart your character, your manliness (and we can add, womanliness). It will undermine your mission and your ability to contribute to the greater good of society or of your community.

Throughout history, sailors have left for the high seas with their communities coming come down to the harbor to bid them off.

Women would be crying as their men stole one last kiss before boarding the ship. "Don't go! You might die in the ocean and perish!"

Those sailors who said, "I have to defend the homeland," or, "I have to trade and bring commerce to our community," were essentially saying, "It's my mission. I have to go."

They knew that they could die in battle. They knew that they could shipwreck in a storm. They knew that they could get drunk, puke overboard and fall in.

But those brave sailors who did come home were loved by their communities... and by their women.

And those who stayed... were peeling potatoes.

Therein lies the paradox. The men who relinquished, the men who stayed, the men who did it their women's or even their families' way, were immediately relegated to, what we today call, wimps.

And so it is in business. One wrong client, especially early on in a startup, can throw you off your mission. It can impact profitability, and it can undermine what you really seek to contribute to the greater marketplace.

If your competitive advantage is in a given niche, and a prospective customer asks you to deviate from it, you face a very critical decision.

Sure, if many customers are demanding something with enhancements – and you can efficiently tweak it, stay passionate about it and drive your business through the roof with it – go for it!

But if you bend to a prospect's whim, if a given customer that isn't your heart's desire pulls you off your strategic center and you take it just for an early deal or cash flow, you could end up with business that simply is not profitable. In broader terms, the marketplace might get the wrong image of what you stand for, and even lose respect in you.

Even worse, you may lose respect in yourself.

The sailor who never left port will always crave the high seas, let alone the respect of his woman and the community at large.

The musician who, at the insistence of his wife for a steady salary, stopped playing with the band to manage his father's hardware store, will always cringe when he sees his buddies rockin' the house on Saturday night. Maybe his buddies will hit fame, fortune and world tours, or maybe they'll just have decades of fun playing at clubs out and about the town and country. "But those big city lights will never be for me."

The woman who stalled her career, due to pressure from her husband and not for her own reasons, will never get it out of her mind… or her heart.

The company that drops its proverbial trousers to get a deal, the startup that strays from its higher mission to serve the wrong customer, almost always regrets it.

More than one CEO of a startup that lost its way can cite a specific deal where *we sold our souls.*

Don't sell out your brand soul for just any client. Stay on strategy. Seek worthy clients who believe in you, your brand and your mission.

To thine own self be true,
And it must follow, as the night the day,
Thou canst not be false to any man.
    -   *Shakespeare*

If Bill were alive today, he'd say, "Stay true to your mission, and you will be loved by the marketplace."

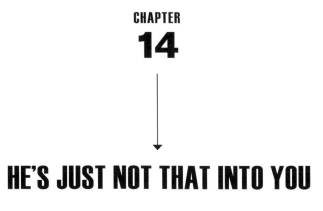

HE'S JUST NOT THAT INTO YOU

You've seen it happen to others more than once.

Maybe you've experienced it first hand and don't want to even admit it.

Because… it… hurts.

It hurts when you fall for someone who doesn't fall for you.

Bad enough is being smitten for someone who has given you the time of day but won't give you her phone number.

Worse is being entirely smitten for someone, wining him, dining her or, yes, giving him sex, only to be called last minute when he just wants a little wham, bam, thank you, m'am… someone who just doesn't give you the love you need.

Greg Behrendt and Liz Tuccillo wrote, *He's Just Not That Into You: The No Excuses Truth to Understanding Guys.* Anecdotally, it was later made into a movie, but the real wisdom can be found in the 2004 book, which was originally written for women, but, here again, applies as much to men.

The idea for *He's Just Not That Into You* took root when Behrendt, a consultant for the TV series *Sex And The City*, was asked by two of the show's women co-writers for advice about a date one of them had had.

After listening to the woman describe the painfully slow developments of a hoped-for romance, Behrendt quipped, "He's just not that into you!"

And so, the book took root, and so did lots of advice about moving on and pursuing the right kind of guy.

The core message of the book, in fact, aligns with another chapter in David Deida's aforementioned, *The Way of the Superior Man*.

Don't fall in love with someone who won't fall in love with you.

You will get pulled off your spiritual center. Your energy will get needlessly sucked away. You will lose other opportunities.

It just sucks.

As a lover, you've only got one life to live.

As a salesperson, you've only got one marketplace to serve.

Trying to satisfy toxic clients who don't see your full value-add and pursuing disinterested prospects who don't move forward in a substantive way brings opportunity costs.

No matter how much *love* you show them, no matter how much you do your very best for them, they don't give you the love… and respect… you deserve.

You'll be kissing their asses, and they will ask you to keep kissing… *and* they will insist it be done a certain way, lest they break up with you, divorce you, fire you.

Like falling for a partner who doesn't love you, chasing clients who don't know what they want in a vendor – or who, as individuals in a business environment, are more concerned with covering their asses internally than they are with driving their business effectively through constructive collaboration – is bad for your karma.

It's also bad for business. These clients are also usually the least profitable ones. Not only do they make you work beyond the agreed scope without additional compensation, they pull you off center.

Like many lovers, many salespeople don't worry about opportunity costs. Nor do many small companies and independent consultants. However, CFO's of major corporations do.

This is where the long-held best practice of *qualifying your leads* comes in. The basics of qualifying go deeper than just assessing if you're talking to the right individual within an organization, or if they're motivated to buy and have the budget at their discretion to back it.

Effective qualifying includes analyzing if the partnership is going to be a good match. Sure, if you're a startup or a first-time freelancer, it's tempting to take whatever business comes along. If you're lonely and haven't had sex or a romantic partner in a long time, it's also tempting to *take what you can get*.

Neediness is not good in love, and it's not good in business.

It's vital to politely dig, to assess if the client is committed to spending the human capital to support you in implementing your value-add effectively and successfully. It's vital to determine if the client has the maturity, yes, *the emotional maturity*, to manage a healthy relationship.

It's vital to get phone calls returned from buyers if you plan to spend time developing a sale with them. It's vital that they contribute to the next steps.

When that stops happening, it's important to realize that they're just not that into you.

Hold your head up, and move on.

CHAPTER

15

$$\downarrow$$

BUT SHE'S OUT OF MY LEAGUE

So this guy walks into a bar.

He's a divorced father, and he's with his son to celebrate the son's rite of passage. It's the son's birthday, and the son is now of legal drinking age.

The father orders two beers.

"Cheers, buddy! I love you, and I wish you health and happiness."

They cling their glasses and slosh down their first gulp, just as three young women walk by. The father smiles confidently, and one of the ladies smiles back before giggling with her friends.

"Now we can start fighting over women, I guess," the father says.

The son laughs and cracks, "No contest!"

"That's the spirit!" the father replies, and clings his son's beer glass again.

"Let me ask you, buddy," the father continues. "Which one of the three floats your boat?"

The son doesn't hesitate. "The one on the right. The one who smiled at you."

"Yeah, young man, you've got good taste. Very good taste. But a minute ago you said, 'No contest,' and now you're noting that she gave *me* the smile. That's only because I looked her in the eye and smiled. So, buddy, don't ever hesitate to smile and say hello to a woman like that. It's that simple."

"Be real, dad. She's out of my league."

"*What? Don't be ridiculous!* I thought your mother was out of my league when I met her, ok?"

"Really?"

"Of course! Even if only for a moment. I had that twinge of, 'Who, me?' But it was only a twinge. I knew I had to dismiss it if I was going to get anywhere with her."

The father wondered if his son was pondering that his own existence was thanks to his father having the balls to approach his mother, or if his son was wondering if he really could get a woman like the one on the right… a woman who he would be just crazy about every day.

"OK, buddy. Here's the deal," the father continued. "You don't want to wake up every day, married to a woman who you believe you *settled* for. Because you'll never stop thinking of the woman whom you had a killer crush on, but thought was *out of your league*. That's not happiness, buddy, and it's not healthy, either!

"Your mom and I had problems those last few years, but that wasn't the cause of it. We were crazy about each other, and we gave it our best. That's a hell of a lot different than settling for second best, and waking up to that every day. Every relationship has problems, but when you're crazy about your partner, you'll work harder on those problems."

The son digested the words, as he looked in the direction where the three ladies had disappeared into the crowd.

"Maybe I'm getting ahead of myself," the father made one last point. "Even early on in a relationship, and actually every day and night, you want to be excited about seeing her. And that's what will make her look forward to being with you."

It's the same with customers. Identify your A-Level Prospects, and go after them… with passion and heartfelt desire.

No prospect is out of your league unless you believe it. This is one of the biggest self-limiting beliefs of start-ups and under-performing salespeople alike.

"They're out of our league."

That's self-limiting. That's bullshit!

Go after your A-Level Prospects. Love them from the moment you call them and every moment thereafter… when you meet them for the first time, when you engage them, when you close them and when you service them.

Bring these customers your best stuff. Challenge their thinking if you think it's flawed, because you respect them, because you love them. If you're crazy about them, they will respect you… and they will love you back.

Very often, clients think they know the solution they're looking for and seek a certain type of vendor. Maybe it's *Big Company* seeking a big vendor, where they'll get the same ol' iceberg lettuce. And until they meet the *Nimble & Edgy Agency*, who has the *confidence* to call them and approach them, *Big Company* will settle for the status quo.

Then they meet you, *Nimble & Edgy*, the right vendor, the right *partner*. You help *Big Company* see things differently, and sometimes you almost can't believe your own good luck. You had a twinge of doubt that *Big Company* was out of your league, but you smiled, looked them in the eyes, introduced yourselves, and a great conversation broke out. Now, you've won their hearts, and you're the happiest little agency in the world.

In the movie, *Hitch, The Love Doctor,* Will Smith plays a dating coach in New York who has some pretty pitiful clients in the form of bachelors longing for love and failing at dating.

In one scene, Hitch, tells his client, Albert, to go after Allegra, who is stunning, just plain awesome and, on paper, definitely out of his league.

He's telling this Average Joe client that if he's confident and charming, Miss Incredible will more likely see his love-worthy qualities.

"Even a beautiful woman doesn't know what she wants... until she sees it."

The beautiful ones... and we shall not overrate physical beauty... the *special* ones, the ones who you might think are *out of your league*, are the ones to build a life with or, at very least, to pursue.

Of course, this is great advice for women, too. And it is of paramount importance for salespeople and entrepreneurs.

The special prospects, the ones who have a special vision, the ones who are executing extraordinarily... those are the ones to build your business with.

If the strategic fit is there, if you can woo them, stay true to your mission and be true to thine own self, by all means, go after these prospects.

No one is out of your league!

Especially those who float your boat! They're the ones you will love doing business with and, it will follow, the ones you will bring the most value to.

A year later, the son introduced his father to his first girlfriend.

His father had to keep his jaw from dropping when he first looked at her. She was… drop… dead… gorgeous. And she had the personality of sunshine in the spring.

At one point, the father whispered to his son, "Dude! She's out of George *Clooney's* league."

His son mischievously smiled back, "Well she's not out of *mine!*"

REGRET IS MORE PAINFUL THAN REJECTION

"We had intense eye contact," she said.

"He smiled at me on the subway platform and looked away. When he looked back, I smiled at him and looked away. This happened a few more times over the next few minutes. I could feel he was as attracted to me as I was to him.

"Then a train pulled up to the platform, and he boarded it. He sat in the window, right in front of where I was standing, looking out at me as the train pulled away... and he was gone.

"The next day at the same time, I came back to the platform... hoping. I know it sounds crazy, but I even came back a few times over the next week or so at that same time. But he was really gone.

"I'll forever wonder why he didn't act. And I'll forever regret that I didn't."

The reason neither she nor he acted was simple: fear of rejection.

As psychologist Sian Bellock's 2011 article in *Psychology Today* outlined, the feeling of rejection is so intense within humans that it can actually transcend our emotional state and become *physically painful*.

This gives new meaning to the idea that *love hurts*.

The intensity varies, and different types of rejection don't always cause physical pain. Yet the fact remains, the emotional pain of social rejection is so intense that it causes many people to avoid taking certain risks.

Even though there is no real, physical danger in starting a conversation with someone who smiles at you on a train platform, or even in calling a new prospect for the first time, the possibility that we may be socially rejected inhibits many people from going out on such limbs.

With this possibility for *rejection* at the forefront, and with the above-mentioned *pain factor* deep in our psyche, the potential reward is not enough to move people many people out of their comfort zone and into the flirt zone.

Many client account people are comfortable at servicing clients.

When the company leadership asks these account people to pursue new business opportunities, be it with potential new clients or even upselling existing ones, most of these people resist.

Their expressed reasons are many. Yet their implicit reason is fear of rejection.

Psychologists call this self-limiting behavior.

Self-limiting behavior is entirely human. It happens to everyone.

Conquering self-limiting fears, however, can unleash new potential for SMEs and independent service providers alike.

The first step is mindset, but changing mindset can be a temporary thing if it's not reinforced with the right skills. Deploying proven best practices in prospecting will bring you rewards. It will bring you early successes that will, in turn, reinforce the mindset and ignite a virtuous cycle.

Suzanne Muller-Heinz is a dating and love life coach in Zurich, and author of *Loveable – 21 Practices for Being in a Loving & Fulfilling Relationship*.

She often tells her clients not to try to eliminate the fear of rejection, but to bravely work through it. Her advice is paradoxical.

"Be afraid and do it anyway," says Muller-Heinz. "Then you'll celebrate in the excitement of 'I did it!' Even if you're unsuccessful, you'll absolutely feel good about having done it. And you *might* even be successful the first time… and you *will* be successful the second or third time, if you do it even half-right!"

Muller-Heinz knows the sales side of this, too. Years ago, she sold hardware in Colorado for a California-based IT company. At first she hated cold calling and prospecting. Then she started celebrating each call regardless of the outcome, and her luck changed.

"It's far better to approach someone and get rejected than it is to be left alone and wondering, in sales and in dating!" says Muller-Heinz.

"You've got little or nothing to lose, and everything to win," she says. "And you won't be left with the pain of wondering about what could have been."

Indeed, regret is more painful than rejection.

Go for it, and then – win, lose or draw – celebrate your courage.

17

DON'T BE BETTER. BE DIFFERENT.

Being better than your competition is certainly better than being equal, which is certainly better than being worse.

But *better* is ethereal. It often doesn't last long, and it's difficult to continually substantiate in your buyer's mind.

Even if you were *the best* yesterday, it doesn't mean you'll be the best today. The competition always moves fast, whether it's in introducing a product that's better than yours or simply in creating the *perception* that their product is better.

Look what happened to *Yahoo!* Once seen as the gold standard in search engines, *Yahoo!* got its proverbial ass kicked by *Google*, who simply did it better, to the point that *google* is now both a proper noun and a verb. *To google* is part of the online vernacular.

But *Google* hasn't settled for just being better. They've moved into areas that *Yahoo!* never dreamed of: *Google Docs, Google Hangouts* and *Google+*. To keep the customers' love, *Google* evolved from *better* to *different*.

It's like dating… and personal branding.

InterNations is a huge social network in major cities around the world. It appeals to expats, or international people who, for professional or personal reasons, move to a foreign city.

Zurich is one of the cities where *InterNations* grew exponentially from 2011 to 2012, and it was loaded with professional people.

Typical conversation at an *InterNations* Zurich event was, "I saw you at the last event, but didn't get a chance to chat. It was so crowded. What do you do?"

"I'm a banker."

Or, "I work for a multi-national as a personal assistant to the Head of Marketing, but I'm looking to grow. I want to move into event marketing."

Or, "Blah, blah, bloody, blah, blah."

In a room full of people with similar professional levels, how do you answer that?

"Cool. I think you deserve a promotion." Duh!

Most people come to *InterNations* events directly from work, and most of the crowd dresses the corporate image. Some aren't even corporate types, but they dress the part, anyway, even though there is no formal dress code. Perhaps they don't want to stand out.

The kiss of death! Not wanting to stand out! Try to be all things to all people, and you'll be nothing to everybody.

Stand out! Niche thyself!

To many people, niching seems risky. They believe that the mainstream is where the action is, and that if they niche themselves, they'll miss opportunities.

Wrong!

The bizarre thing is, if you asked seven out of ten people at *InterNations* Zurich why they are even there, it isn't to network for a new job. It's to meet new people and, oh, yeah, to find a romantic partner.

But here they are, trying to be *better* than half of the other people in the room. What would prompt a *romantic* prospect to take a date with one cookie cutter executive type or the other?

But a few are different. Whether they dress casually, or whether they talk about their non-professional interests, they're different.

So how about this?

"I saw you at the last event, but didn't get a chance to chat. It was so crowded. What do you do?"

"Outside of work, I'm working on my Italian. On many weekends I go to a cute little *albergo* outside of Lugano. In fact, I'm leaving the office early Friday and heading straight there."

Imagine the possibilities for a suitor to build on that line, to enquire more, to be *really interested*?

Imagine how *different*?

While both men and women show up at such events (and go through *life!*) with a predetermined profile of a romantic partner they'd like to meet, the fact is, when they meet that profile, they often don't think it's *good enough*, and they hold out for somebody *better*.

Then they meet someone *different*, and they are attracted. The predetermined profile goes right out the window!

Great marketers know that it's not just a quality game. It's a differentiation game, too.

Apple, for example, never built its messaging around being better. In the early days of *Apple*, Steve Jobs himself said, "How does somebody know what they want when they've never even seen it?"

That sounds a bit like *Hitch, The Love Doctor's* aforementioned advice to Albert.

Jobs' mantra, from building *Apple* in the '80s to its resurgence a decade ago, was always, "We don't want to be better. We want to be different."

Don't be better. Be different.

Stand for something different.

Then see how quickly your conversations start and how engaging they become.

18

TAKE MY BREATH AWAY

"One dance is all we get."

Wise words again, from *Hitch, The Love Doctor.*

Early in a sale, emotions sell.

Granted, it's incumbent upon the salesperson to say the right things mentally, rationally and professionally, but successful salespeople also inspire emotionally.

Take my breath away!

Early on, that's what customers subconsciously want you to do – to take their breath away, to seduce them.

They want a vision of an ideal future. They want a knight in shining armor.

Early on, they do not identify the white knight with final contract negotiations. All that complexity comes later. If you don't inspire them early, if you don't seduce them, your chances of moving forward are reduced.

But if you *do* take their breath away, if early in their purchasing process, you seduce them and touch them at a deep, emotional level, they'll more likely be motivated to go further with you later… to engage more deeply.

Indeed, most deals today become complex later in the sales cycle. Challenges arise. By having a strong emotional connection firmly embedded in the buyer's heart, you will more likely be able to overcome these challenges. Emotions play a powerful role in human reasoning, so hooking the customer early is critical.

This is not to say you should pitch a CEO with something like, "Stay with your feelings here." No way!

Triggering a prospect's emotions requires speaking her professional language and being relevant to her needs, while striking at the heart of what her drivers are.

"We believe we can increase your sales by 15 percent."

That is not irrelevant poetry, by any means. To the CEO or the Head of Sales and Marketing, this will sound professional while potentially striking an emotional chord. Her curiosity will be piqued. Her attention will be focused on you, and her imagination may start to wander toward the promised land.

In a professional sense, you want to take her breath away.

So, why bury the heart stopper?

Why not seduce the customer into the beginning of a love affair with the first dance?

As Scarlett told Ripcord in the 2009 film, *G.I. Joe: The Rise of the Cobra*, "Attraction is an emotion."

Scarlett isn't the only one saying this. Psychologists and dating coaches confirm that we are usually not consciously aware when we are attracted. In the first moments, attraction is purely emotional.

Emotions are triggered, and they often trigger us into action.

And here's the golden nugget. The most effective way to trigger emotions in others is to keep… it… simple.

Emotions are *only* triggered through *simplicity*.

If you're hiking in the Rocky Mountains and a grizzly bear steps into your trail, you've got a problem on your hands. There's nothing complex about it. Your attention has been grabbed, and it's 100 per cent emotional. It's not likely that you'll look at your partner and say, "I think I'll text message the office and see how they're doing on the Asian project," or, "Do you think we should refinance the house?"

If a prospective buyer is urgently looking for a solution to streamline costs, and you say, "We helped a company of your size cut 20 per cent from their overseas logistics and operations," you will have their immediate attention.

Again, that sounds rational and, in fact, it is. You're talking their language and you're addressing their needs. You're in their sweet spot.

This is why it is also emotionally triggering. They'll most likely be leaning forward. Their vision will narrow.

The emotional trigger may then prompt subconscious thoughts like, "Hmmm, these folks could help us hit our targets. Let's go deeper with this conversation. Let's engage."

Striking an emotional chord does not guarantee that you will close any and every deal. Deals become more rational, analytical and mental as they progress and, yes, complexity will sooner or later enter the picture.

But if you don't seduce a prospect early on, if you don't grab a prospect's curiosity with a clear vision of an ideal future, with a *simple* value-add, with something *different* from the rest, then your chances of progressing are much lower than if you do.

Simplicity sells.

Simplicity triggers emotions. Emotions motivate us to action, even if that emotion is curiosity and the action is to learn more. That's a great start!

If you're a divorced mom and have had eye contact a few times with an interesting looking man at the supermarket, and then you see him at the high school concert with kids the same age as yours and no wife on the horizon, you'll be curious.

If a mutual friend then tells you, "He separated two years ago," you might not notice that heart of yours skipping a beat, those pupils of yours dilating or that breath of yours being taken away.

Emotions cause physical change in the body. That's how powerful they are.

If your mutual friend goes on to say, "He's a really good father, too. He jumped out of the corporate world after the separation to spend more time with his kids. He's got his priorities straight... and I don't think there's a lady in his life," you might not notice that body language of yours completely change.

Curiosity is piqued. Attraction is set on fire. Vision narrows.

The object of desire is the only thing you can concentrate on.

Interest is established, and this draws you deeper into engagement.

This is how romance starts.

And this is how many successful sales start.

Keep it relevant and professional, but find a link with something that appeals emotionally with each customer early on. Find their hot buttons.

Again, Shakespeare said it best. "Who has loved who has not loved at first sight?"

CHAPTER
19

PRE-SELECTION & THE WING MAN

John was looking forward to this month's networking event. Two months earlier, he had chatted with Theresa and was attracted to her. She was, in his eyes, both beautiful and down-to-earth.

He had to miss the following month's event due to business travel and, over the online platform, he saw that Theresa had confirmed her attendance. He posted on the event forum that he would miss everybody, and then sent Theresa a direct message saying, "Have fun," along with a little joke about yoga that he remembered from their conversation.

She sent him a direct message reply. "Your energy will be here even if you're not. Safe travels home."

John's heart skipped a beat when he read that, but he didn't want to appear too needy, so he only sent back a smiley.

When this month's event was posted online, Theresa confirmed within a few hours, and John confirmed a few hours after that.

When John arrived that evening, he saw Theresa talking to a guy. Nevertheless, she smiled and nodded. So John smiled and gave a small wave from across the room, then greeted the gregarious event organizer with a big hug, who introduced John to a woman new to the network.

John gladly chatted with her for a while, and then invited another man and woman to join them.

Theresa, meanwhile, was still chatting with the same guy.

Another half-hour later, John was again on the move, joining his fourth circle. He couldn't help but think, "That guy hanging on Theresa has good taste, damn it. But he's doing it all wrong."

Fifteen minutes later, John saw that Theresa was standing alone, and she smiled. John excused himself from his circle and made his way over to Theresa.

They chatted for a few minutes before *the guy* came back, so John greeted him with a smile, as Theresa introduced him as David.

David started talking again to Theresa and squared his shoulders to face her directly. Clearly, he didn't want John in his territory.

John touched Theresa on the elbow and said, "We'll catch up." She touched the back of John's forearm as he walked away, and David seemed to take little notice of John's departure.

Was John upset with David?

Absolutely not.

John felt more confident than ever. Within two steps of Theresa and David, he started a conversation with a woman whom, to John's good fortune, was then joined by her girlfriend.

And so it continued.

And so David continued to talk to Theresa, his shoulders remaining squared on her. Theresa, however, was now clearly opening her body positioning toward the rest of the room. She nodded as David continued to talk to her, but John could see she wanted to mingle.

John was on the move again. This time he started chatting with three men who were, in fact, joking that the prettiest woman at the event, Theresa, was being monopolized by "that guy," David.

One even said, "He's hopeless."

"But he's getting her number now," another one said. David and Theresa had their mobile phones out.

The crowd began to thin, so John made his way over to the event host to say good night.

And so did Theresa.

"Well, I'm going to be leaving soon," John said to both of them, and shook the host's hand.

"Yes, me, too," Theresa said. "Oh my god, my train is leaving in ten minutes!"

"I'll walk you there," John said.

They grabbed their coats and walked swiftly toward the train station, at times trotting, laughing all the way.

On the platform, they gave a kiss on the cheek, and Theresa held John's shoulder for an extra micro-second.

"Glass of wine early next week?" John asked.

"That would be nice," Theresa smiled. "Here's my number… and my train is leaving!" she laughed running toward the door.

John watched her train depart, Theresa waving and smiling from the window.

As the train disappeared, John sent her a text message. "And here's my number :-) You're a good runner. As to that glass of wine, Friday 8 pm, Pier 41?"

Theresa replied to John immediately. "Yes. 8:30 :-)"

Theresa also had a text message from David. "Great seeing you tonight. What are you doing Friday evening?"

Theresa answered David the next morning. "Sorry, I have plans. Let's have coffee next time you're in Zurich."

Did Theresa choose John because his text beat David's?

No way.

Women know what they want, and they'll break a date if they want somebody else more.

And what they want more than a large bank account, six-pack abs or a guy who loves kids is… a guy that other women want.

It's that simple.

It's called *Pre-Selection.*

David apparently had no clue of the Pre-Selection laws of biology. If he did, he didn't deploy them.

Once he had cornered Theresa, the apple of his and everyone else's eye, he failed by suffocating her.

David further failed by displaying potential insecurity in not letting her go, in cutting off John and in positioning himself to not welcome anyone else into their conversation.

And where David failed *miserably* was by not showing in any way, shape or form, that other women in the room found him nice... eligible... or desirable.

This is not just human psychology. This is biology.

In many animal species, like guppies, the females have a biological desire to have their eggs fertilized by well-shaped, brightly colored males.

This sex appeal is not just visual taste. It's not just eye candy for the underwater world. This is about finding a mate who will provide strong and healthy offspring.

Once again, it's about *survival* of the species and the *thrival* of the clan... the nest!

When mating season comes around, the healthier and feistier guppy chicks lead the way in having their eggs fertilized first. They narrow down a shortlist of bright and healthy guppy dudes, and they start the Request For Proposal process. They do this by showing their interest in, say, four or five of the brightest and healthiest dudes.

Among these four or five lucky dudes, the differences and distinctions begin to blur. None of these feisty guppy chicks are able make up their mind as to which guppy dude is the hottest.

Who will be the male finalist? Who will be the lucky guppy?

The final decision of *first mate* selection remains in a holding pattern until… drum roll, please… *one* of the dominant females can't contain her horniness any longer and commits to *one* of the bright males… *any* one from the shortlist.

Lo and behold, once one female commits, once she says, "He's the hottie," so then do the rest. All of the feistier females immediately throw themselves at that male's, um, dorsal fins.

Imagine the action this lucky guppy dude gets!

In typical animal kingdom behavior, the lucky male probably has enough feist for more than one female. It's not until he spends his energy… and his fertilizer, so to say… that he buggers off, grabs a beer and watches guppy football. (Not that he'd go fishing.) And so, the chosen one is out for the season.

For all the remaining guppy chicks that have not yet released their tummy of guppy caviar, the selection ritual starts again. Who will be the runner up?

Here again, among the remaining, most colorful male guppies, the next one to get the *fertilize me* action is the one that is somehow desired by the first guppy female to get weak in the fins and commit to him.

What is it about the chosen dude that causes the first, horny guppy chick to put her chips on red?

No one knows, but, again, once one female commits to that male, the other females swarm him.

That's *Pre-Selection*. It's the biological phenomenon in which a male is deemed desirable by females merely because other females desire him.

Now, ladies, before you go get your, um, nickers in a twist, admit it. You play a similar game… at least the savvy among you do.

That game actually has a chick's dating book named after it, *Always Hit On The Wing Man*, by Jake, a ghost name for editors at *Glamour* Magazine.

It goes like this, ladies. You're at a pub or an event. You spot a guy you like, and he's with a male friend. When a conversation starts, you greet both of them, but you don't show your warmth and charm immediately toward the apple of your eye, but rather, to the apple of your eye's *friend*.

If the guy you really want is, indeed, interested in you, by you showing your interest to the other guy, you'll entice the apple of your eye more *and*... he'll have to up his game.

He'll have to visibly show you he's interested in *you*. He'll have to work hard. As the old saying goes, he'll have to make a fool of himself for love, and compete with his friend.

Maybe *Pre-Selection* and *The Wing Man* fall into the simple economics of supply and demand, and the psychology of perceived abundance and scarcity. Either way, it's human and animal behavior that is at work, timelessly and universally.

As such love… *and* sales… are all about behavior.

Several years ago I worked with a startup in Zurich that had strong funding and a driven CEO.

Early on, the CEO put together a first-class sales organization that was lean 'n mean, and he worked with them every day.

It wasn't quick and it wasn't easy, but long before the investors started yelping, the startup secured a great customer with a great brand name. And then another.

A week ago, as I write these lines, I bumped into the two main salespeople.

Oh, man! These guys looked the part. These guppy dudes were bright and healthy. Really. They looked masculine. They dressed professionally. They exuded confidence and charm.

And they were doing more deals.

So I asked them. "If you could tell me one thing, outside of your sales abilities, what is the *one thing* that's driving your sales now?"

Without hesitation, the more senior sales guy said, "Momentum. Getting our first deal was a struggle. But once we got the bank as our first client, we got the next four deals in two months. Those four were in the pipeline, but it was like everyone was waiting for someone to bite first."

"Pre-Selection," I explained.

"Absolutely," the second sales gunslinger said. "Now we're working on a new round of deals, and they're moving more quickly than the first. The marketplace perceives us as hot stuff, and we're striking while the iron's hot."

Back to Theresa on the train, taking a date with John and not with David.

Theresa *pre-eliminated* David. He had monopolized her time at the event and he had demonstrated insecurity and possessiveness. He was not seen as being desired by other women. He was not seen as a hot property out in the marketplace.

John, on the other hand, consciously or otherwise, worked the Pre-Selection concept effectively. If it was conscious, he tactically executed well. If it was unconscious, then John's simply a secure, confident guy.

And that's what women biologically want in men *and* that's what more modern men want in women. Psychologists overwhelmingly claim that if there's one thing that pre-selects the Pre-Selection process above anything else, it's confidence.

Customers like confident salespeople.

They like to engage with salespeople who have all the soft skills, including confidence.

Sure, they want products and services that perform well, and having a growing portfolio of happy customers, being a hot property, speaks volumes out in the marketplace.

This drives buyer attraction *and* trust.

The first moral of this story skews towards marketing. Testimonials matter.

The marketplace doesn't always hear about your successes. So blow your horn online, in press releases and in customer conversations.

This is, of course, a challenge if you're a startup and don't have any concluded deals to announce. So stay confident and tell prospects whom you're flirting with. The more customer conversations you have, the more you can genuinely tell these stories and, of course, the more likely you'll convert the first one.

The second moral of this story is all about sales skills and hiring good salespeople.

Train them. Good sales skills translate to confidence.

If you're a salesperson, get trained or insist on being trained.

Be confident, and be charming.

W. Anton is the author of *The Manual: What Women Want And How To Give It To Them*.

This is not a book for the light-hearted, but it also not a book on the shallow art of picking up women. It's a book on how to get dates and have successful relationships.

Anton bases the book on three pillars: confidence, charm and responsibility.

To be successful with women, a man must first be confident in himself. Some men don't have this inner-confidence but, Anton writes, if this is the case, *acting* confident is key. Then with time, the outer confidence seeps inward. This then translates to being genuinely confident in approaching women and initiating relationships.

Secondly, Anton claims, a man must be charming. Confidence should enable a man to be charming, to making the woman feel attractive, interesting and that she's the apple of his eye.

Then, as much as women today *might* take the lead in asking a man for his phone number, asking him out or inviting him over for dinner, a man shouldn't rely on it. If a man wants to be romantically successful, he must assume the responsibility to keep the relationship moving forward.

Take these three above points and change the Martian *man* to *salesperson*, and change the Venusian *woman* to *customer*.

Doesn't that sound like great selling, too?

Customers may believe they want any salesperson who offers the best product. And rationally, they actually do.

But remember, as Dale Carnegie said, we're emotional creatures. That includes customers. Customers are in *Pre-Selection* mode and they're usually not even aware of it.

As marketers and salespeople, we must be aware of it and exercise it. We should say the things and do the things that earn us *Pre-Selection* status. We shouldn't be shy that we've been hitting on the wingman, that we're actively securing a portfolio of great customers.

Pre-Selection and *The Wing Man* won't close the deal. But it will seduce high-quality prospects. It will open relationships with higher quality buyers. It will bring the *Good Housekeeping* Seal of Approval.

It won't guarantee a hot weekend in a beach house with the apple of your eye. It won't guarantee a happy-ever-after wedding with European royalty.

But it will put you in the game, the dating game or the sales game, with higher quality targets, and more of them.

John and Theresa don't go to as many events any more, because they've moved in together. David is still single.

↓

CHAPTER 20

THE STRENGTH OF WEAK TIES

"If your house burns down, you'll probably move in with strong ties," says Howard Rheingold.

"But," Rheingold adds, "you'll probably meet your life partner through weak ties," especially as you move past your 20's and into your 30's and beyond.

Rheingold is author of an array of books over three decades, including the 2002 *Smart Mobs: The Next Social Revolution* and the 2012 *Net Smart: How To Thrive Online.*

Like anything social, online human behavior mirrors offline human behavior.

Why do so many single people find love at other people's weddings?

Indeed, weddings provide romantic settings, lots of people dressed to the nines, lots of drinking and lots of dancing.

But the big reason so many single people find love at weddings is because they meet people whom they haven't met before.

For any one person in attendance, at least half of the other attendees can usually be categorized as weak ties.

Let's say that the bride and the groom met at college. Attending the wedding will typically be friends, family and loved ones from two different hometowns, that of the bride's and that of the groom's, in addition to the friends from the one university.

Bang! Lot's of new connections. Lots of people meeting each other for the first time.

Let's go one step further. Let's say that the bride and the groom meet early in their careers, after university. Attending the wedding will be friends, family and loved ones from the two different hometowns, as well as friends from the two universities and the city or region where they both work.

Exponential bang! Lots *more* people meeting each other for the first time.

This is the strength of weak ties.

A wedding of *strong ties* would be one where the bride and groom met in high school, and most of the wedding guests are from that same town. This doesn't kill new hookups, but the potential for new hookups is much smaller.

After the age of 25, we rarely meet *the one* through close ties, through people with whom we have long-established relationships. Their circles are too closely similar to our circles, so no new action happening there!

Weak-tie environments are where the higher-probability action is.

And so it is in sales.

The savvy salesperson will not attend just his industry's annual convention. He'll go to events of other industries.

As an example, the sports marketing industry has numerous conferences. In North America, IEG is the gold standard conference dedicated to sponsorship.

The successful sponsorship salespeople go there. They might gain valuable intelligence. They might get future speaking engagements. They will strengthen existing relationships, but they will meet only a few new sponsorship buyers each year.

This an industry of strong ties, at least for the sponsorship salesperson. The contacts are many, but the real sales opportunities are few and far between, because many salespeople and prospects already know each other.

Some really successful and savvy sponsorship salespeople go to conventions *outside* of the sports sponsorship industry.

They go to auto shows. They go to telecom conventions. They go to travel shows.

Here they get fresh insights. They learn things that catalyze other sponsorship possibilities.

And they meet weaker ties.

They don't meet many people from their own industry, yet they *do* meet a *few*, *new* sponsor prospects, often with marketing and business objectives that are exactly right for a sponsorship property that the sponsorship salesperson might be selling.

Such prospects are often more pre-disposed to being pitched for sponsorships than the ones attending the sponsorship conferences.

Apply this to your industry. As a salesperson, expand the concept of conferences to whatever business circle applies.

If you're single and looking for the love of your life, pass on the annual cookout at your best friend's place and go to your second cousin's wedding on the other side of the country.

If you're selling something, re-consider the industry in which you sell.

This is the paradox of social and business circles when it comes to finding new opportunities.

Strong ties bring fewer opportunities.

Weak ties bring more opportunities.

Pursue networks of weak ties, and opportunities will become more abundant.

↓

CHAPTER 21

NETWORKING & SOCIALIZING: MAKE A FOOL OF YOURSELF FOR LOVE

So you're at an event of weak ties, with so many people you've never met. Now what?

Are you afraid of making a fool of yourself?

The paradox *here* is that by playing it safe and not risking making a fool of yourself, you actually look, or at very least feel, more foolish. It's simply foolish to go to a networking event and not network.

More than one woman has said she loves it when a man makes a fool of himself for love.

Perhaps Veronica Chambers, features director at *Glamour* and author of *The Joy of Doing Things Badly*, says it best. "Making a fool of yourself for love is ultimately about you, how much you have to give and the distances you will travel to keep your heart wide open when everything around you makes you feel like slamming it shut and soldering it closed."

That's right. Along with confidence and charm, nothing attracts more than a generous heart. People love it when you take the risk of reaching out to them, be it for love or for business.

The response one gets from making an approach to any given love interest or a potential business lead will vary, but one thing is clear: those who approach, and those who are approachable, find more opportunities and better opportunities over time than those who appear nervous.

Whether it be an event or an impromptu moment like standing in the line at the supermarket, the choice is yours. Connect, or wait for others to connect.

The former takes a little courage, but brings the best results. The latter is easy, but your destiny is not in your hands.

Trea Tijmens is a professional matchmaker and dating coach based in Geneva and co-author of *Sexy Secrets to a Juicy Love Life*. She's also in business for herself. She feels strongly that pro-actively making connections brings clear benefits to her dating clients, as well as to her own business development.

Trea has many best practices that she recommends to her single clients that apply to meeting new people - whether at events, the supermarket, airports or just about anywhere. Below are six of them.

Claim Responsibility

You are responsible for the success of your networking. You are responsible for making the networking experience positive. Ask not what others can bring you but what you can bring to them.

So, no one is looking at you, smiling at you or talking with you? Do you wish it were different? Then be the change you want to see in others. Look at people, smile and talk. You will be amazed at how contagious this is.

Two Choices: Wait or Create

In sales as in dating, we have two choices: wait for opportunities or create opportunities.

Waiting means that you want something, you have a goal, but that you are not taking action to get to that goal. A goal without action is a dream. Doing nothing usually does not bring us further toward our goal. If we do nothing, nothing will change in our situation.

So we have to become active and initiate opportunities ourselves.

Set The Right Small Goals

Setting goals is great. However, if you are on a mission to sell or find a date, people smell it from miles away. You'll come across as a *closer*, when what you really want to be at this stage is an *opener*.

Instead, set realistic goals, such as I will speak to five new gentlemen. I would like to speak to someone who has a connection in the travel sector. You will be much more likely to achieve your goals, and you will feel confident, energized and motivated to do it again.

Over time, increase your goals. The idea is that you continually expand your comfort zone.

Don't beat yourself up if things do not work the way you would have liked immediately. It's a learning process. Keep tweaking and improving, and you will be successful.

Be Positive

Positive attracts. Confidence attracts.

Smile. Be upbeat, playful and fun. Make others feel good about themselves. Give them sincere compliments.

Be in the moment and give the person you speak to your full attention. Be genuinely interested in the other, not in pushing your own agenda. Look for the good in everyone. Everyone wants to be appreciated and people love to help.

A simple way to engage with someone is to ask for help on something.

"Hello, can you tell me what time the apero / dancing / presentation starts?"

Then, "Thanks so much. By the way, I am Trea," and give them a smile and a warm handshake.

Make It Easy

In addition to being confident in approaching people, make it easy for people to approach you, too.

Position yourself at opportune places where it is easy to make connections, and look at people. Opportune places can be anywhere: close to the food buffet, bar or an entrance where everybody has to pass. Try different locations and see what works. Never hide in a quiet area or dark corner.

And simply don't check messages on your mobile, and don't make phone calls. If you have to make an urgent call or reply to an important message, step away from the high-visibility places.

Otherwise, always be engaged with your environment. Keep your body turned towards others, look at them and just smile.

Just Connect

Connective networking is networking with a purpose but, again, don't show up pushing an obvious agenda.

If you come to a networking event or party with a mission such as "I have to get a new client," or, "I have to find a date tonight," you will be too focused on what *you* want.

Just be in the moment. Enjoy the people, and just connect.

When you make a fool of yourself – for love or for sales – it gets easier the more you do it. When you see how much people appreciate it, you'll actually feel wiser.

When it looks easy for you, and when it feels easy for the others, it's actually not so foolish, after all.

22

ENOUGH ABOUT ME. LET'S TALK ABOUT YOU.

There is no clearly defined line for when one moves from seducing to engaging. Yet for any relationship to move into any depth, engagement is critical.

Seduction alone is for narcissists. Engagement is for those seeking connection and deeper relationships.

Perhaps a way to distinguish between the seduction and engagement processes is, "Keep it simple in marketing. Go deeper in sales."

This is not to call marketers *narcissists*, by any means. The job of marketing, many believe, is to attract qualified leads into the top of the sales cycle. The job of the salesperson is to convert prospects into customers.

But moving from attracting to closing is a long way. There are tools to shorten deal cycles when they are terribly long, but shortcuts are usually shortsighted. *Pitch and close* is outdated and a sure trust-killer.

Engagement is the long road in between where trust is deepened.

At some point, preferably sooner than later, you have to move the conversation away from yourself, your sexy products and your guru-esque management team and toward the customer.

Spend time here. Spend a lot of time talking with the customer about the customer!

So there you are on your first date.

The small talk has been flowing, and your date has shown total interest in that life-defining event of yours.

"Wow!" he says. I can see how this defines you."

So you feel reassured, and you mention how another event in your life has reinforced it.

Stop!

Back up. Let's hit rewind.

"Wow!" he says. I can see how this defines you."

That's exactly when you should hear that little voice in your head say, "Enough about me. Let's talk about you."

So you say, "Yes. Well, we all have defining moments, I guess. How about you?"

Well done!

Your date says, "Well, after I graduated college, I lived for a year in London…"

So you say, "I love London, too! The last time I was there…"

Oops, you did it again.

Shifting the conversation away from yourself and toward your love interest – or customer – is only halfway charming.

No one's perfect at listening, the author included! And yes, we can all occasionally catch ourselves shifting the conversation toward the other person and then jumping back in talking about ourselves as soon as they finish their first sentence.

We're not bad people for doing this. We're comfortable speaking about ourselves because it's charted territory.

Listening to someone else brings you to new, uncharted territory, and that can bring us out of the comfort zone. But listening is charming. It's also the most underrated trust-building tool.

It's great to spark interest by describing that meaningful, life-changing event. It's great to open a sale by going for the heart, by finding that emotional trigger.

But the real engagement app, in sales and in love, is asking great questions.

The purpose of opening is to earn the right to ask questions.

Early in the sales cycle, you often have to open the meeting. You often have to present enough about yourself to show your competence and your value. But your radar should always be on, looking for the opportunity to ask questions to the buyer, about the buyer. You should be *hungry* for the moment in which you've earned the right to ask questions.

Once you've earned it, don't squander it. The value of the questions is for naught if you don't truly listen. Although buyers may expect you to present your services and your capabilities, what they subconsciously want is for you to understand them.

So keep listening. You've earned the right to ask questions, so go deeper with questions and exploration about what you're hearing.

This fosters engagement and builds trust. This gets the buyer to, slowly, fall in love with you.

I was once facilitating a pitch workout with a client in New York.

Early on, several members of the team stated that, in a first meeting, prospective clients expect them to present. However, they also stated that their most productive meetings occur when they never get through their initial presentation.

"When we don't get past the fourth or fifth slide in a pitch, that's when we get the best outcomes. Somehow, early in our presentation, it feels like we're getting sidetracked away from our material and we start talking about what challenges the prospect is experiencing or what opportunities they want to seize. The meeting takes an entirely different course from our planned presentation, and that's when we really get traction."

The two painful words above are "somehow" and "sidetracked."

Moving the conversation away from your sexy products should not *somehow* happen, and it shouldn't feel as though you're getting *sidetracked*. You're *on* track!

So we ran a mock pitch.

About five slides into it, the selling team asked a question. "Is this a challenge that your organization is facing?"

"Yes, definitely!" the mock buyer, a consultant I had hired, replied. "The CEO's been all over my ass, in fact. I've got to make something happen pronto."

You could feel the selling team sense victory. "Oh, well we've got a great solution for you. Let's go forward to Slide 8."

"No!" my consultant shrieked, losing his mock buyer guise. "You listened to us for one answer, and then you moved forward with *your* solution. You know I have a problem, but that's all you know."

"You've got to show us more *love* here," I half-joked. "You guys aren't very charming. You're not gazing into our eyes as we begin to talk about *us*. You're not really listening, baby. You don't understand us, honey. Show us some *love!*"

Many sales have been lost by talking too much. Few have been lost by listening too much.

Buyers today don't want your products. They want your solutions. They want you to help them achieve their dreams.

You will only discover what they are if you listen. You will only engage them if you *really* listen!

Don't be a narcissist.

In romance, women want to be listened to. Men want to feel important. In business, everyone wants to feel understood.

"Listening is a magnetic and strange thing, a creative force. When we are listened to, it makes us unfold and expand."
- Karl Menninger

Asking great questions is the greatest engagement app. Listening is the biggest trust builder.

23

PEEL THE ONION

Karl had a gift of getting prospects and customers to open up. He was skillful in asking good questions, and listening.

He often visited prospects with Richard, the lead product manager of a consulting service. Richard was an expert in his product line, and a great presenter and storyteller.

After one of their early prospect visits together, Karl had some tough love for Richard, some discomforting advice.

"You talk too much."

This was bitter pill for Richard to swallow, especially delivered in that capsule. But he accepted Karl's observation and learned from it. He also agreed to let Karl plan and steer future meetings.

About three months later, they had secured a fair number of second meetings with prospects, but they weren't getting commitments, requests for proposals or even third meetings... until Richard started speaking up again. Richard began dropping in case studies and anecdotes during prospect meetings.

"You're back to your old habits," Karl snarled as they left a second meeting with a prospect. "You did a lot of talking in that meeting."

Richard agreed, but also jousted back. "And they've asked us to present a solution next week. I think what I talked about was necessary.

"In fact," Richard continued, "I presented an idea for addressing their challenge. I started talking because, well, it really felt to me that *you* were asking too many questions."

"But we know that clients like to be listened to," Karl shot back," and that's a trust builder early on."

"I agree. I've learned to do that more, and I absolutely see the benefits in it," Richard said. "But are we still in the *early on* stage? It seems like we're keeping ourselves in the early stages.

"Sorry, Karl," Richard went on. "Sometimes it feels like *all you do* is ask questions – good questions, I agree, but many times it feels like an *interrogation*."

Karl grimaced but didn't say anything.

Richard continued, "Today, we secured the next meeting – to start building a solution together – shortly after I outlined the case study and showed how we would approach their critical issues. At some point, we have to talk about *us*, too... and not just us, but about how we can *help* them. We have to take a stand."

Lorena was really looking forward to her first date with Pascal. They had met briefly at a networking event. At the following month's event, they spent a half-hour chatting and Lorena really opened up.

Pascal was different from other men she had met in this network. He had almost childlike eyes. He showed curiosity for life, not to mention a curiosity for Lorena.

Early in the first date, though, she got spooked. Pascal said very little about himself.

Lorena was definitely talking more than Pascal. His eye contact and smile made it safe for her to do that, but after a while, Lorena was feeling uncomfortable… almost *creepy*.

So she asked a few questions. Pascal answered them briefly, and often followed up with another question. One time Pascal even said, "Your life is so much more interesting than mine. I could listen to you all night."

At that moment, Pascal's smile suddenly seemed disingenuous to Lorena. Her mind started creating weird stories about him. Did this guy have something to hide? If so, what? If he can't talk to me much about his life, how much will I understand what he wants in a relationship? What are his values?

When they were finished with the main course, Lorena passed on dessert. Pascal encouraged her. "I'll have one if you have one. Or we can share one. Whatever you like. Tell me about your favorite desserts."

"I love so many desserts, I don't know how to answer your question, Pascal. But tonight, well, I had something weird for lunch," Lorena lied, "and now it seems to be acting up."

No after-dinner drink at someplace quieter. No kiss on the lips at the tram stop. No second date in the calendar.

Neither Pascal, in his date with Lorena, nor Karl, in his pitching with Richard, effectively peeled the onion. Neither of them offered a little every time they received a little.

Again, listening is an undeniable trust builder. It's charming. It's consultative.

But too much of it can be a turnoff for both buyers and lovers.

Not saying much about *yourself* can be spooky on a date, and it can give the impression of no substance under the surface in a sale.

A great conversation is give-and-take. Talk a little. Listen a little. Then when you talk again, it should have purpose, direction. It should go one layer deeper into the onion.

Peel the onion one layer at a time.

Peeling the onion doesn't have to be exactly 50-50. You're listening 60 percent of the time and talking 40 percent? Great!

But if you're listening 90 percent of the time and talking ten, you might be spooky. You might not be showing substance.

Be interested, but also be interesting.

Peel an onion together, one layer at a time.

↓

MY HERO & YOUR STORY

Harry Potter is my hero.

And the *Harry Potter* series is the most under-recognized love story of our time.

JK Rowling was absolutely masterful in not only using *The Hero's Journey* formula as a highly engaging literary tool, but in using every single word to make one big point… and that point has everything to do with love.

If you use *The Hero's Journey* formula in your storytelling – whether it's an ongoing, unfolding branding story that you'll develop over years or a relatively quick anecdote about why you do what you do – your stories will simply be more compelling.

They will win customers' hearts.

Storytelling has been so hot in the blogosphere over the past five years that it's *almost* an over-used word. The reason storytelling is all the rage these days is because it works.

Stories stick!

Storytelling won't go away any time soon. After all, it's been with us since the caveman. Tales by the campfire. The one that got away. Family history. All wrapped up in stories.

Humans are programmed for stories. Great stories engage our imagination. We participate in them, mentally and emotionally.

"Those who tell stories rule the world."
– Hopi proverb

Those who tell stories capture hearts!

Use stories to peel the onion in your customer engagement, to get customers to fall in love with you.

In its bare bones, a story can be a case study of how a previous client achieved success by working with you.

As in any story, such a case study should have a plot, in which a character overcomes an obstacle. Here's a quick, effective model.

P.O.S.E.
> **P:** Problem
>> • Our client had a certain problem or challenge.
> **O:** Outcome
>> • This is what we achieved for them.
> **S:** Solution
>> • This is how we did it.
> **E:** Essence
>> • And here's the big takeaway.

To be chronological, you could invert the S and the O. So, after stating the Problem, you outline the Solution before the Outcome.

I like the current order, however, for two reasons. Here's the crass one, first. It allows my acronym to form a word you might remember, POSE.

The less crass and more important reason, however, is that the Outcome shows the value that you provided to the previous client.

If, early in a sales call, you boldly state a Value Proposition for focusing your prospect on a vision, an ideal future, then providing the Outcome in a case study isn't going to blow the ending. It states the value that you provided to the previous client. This could take all but 20 seconds.

So to provide a bit more context, let's tell a business case study in the form of children's story. For this, we'll go with the chronological order.

Problem

Once upon a time, there was a company called *Three Little Pigs*. Because of its poor customer service, it was about to be eaten up by *The Big Bad Wolf*, a.k.a. the blogosphere.

Three Little Pigs had a website, a house made of hay, that proclaimed superior products and stellar customer service. The blogosphere not only bashed *Three Little Pigs* on their service problem, they also annihilated them on their lack of responsiveness, for not even listening to the online pork fest.

So *Three Little Pigs* built a house made of sticks, opened a Twitter account and a blog, and they took on *The Big Bad Wolf* bloggers. They showed them that they could be tough, too.

This only made the wolves angrier and more vociferous.

Solution

Three Little Pigs hired us to defend them from *The Big Bad Wolf*. Sure, we built them a house made of bricks, but we actually left the front door open and put out a welcome mat.

We didn't fight *The Big Bad Wolf* bloggers. We embraced them, and showed them that *Three Little Pigs* was listening. We apologized for any shortcomings, and we asked them for recommendations on how to fix our problems.

Outcome

The Big Bad Wolf bloggers were actually nice. They came and went through our open doors as they pleased, and they even gave us suggestions for improvement.

They became our friends, our evangelists, and before long they were actually traveling in wolf packs to our defense. Our customer service improved measurably.

Essence

As a result of working with us, *Three Little Pigs'* perceived customer satisfaction jumped 15 percent in one quarter, when the previous quarter it had dropped by 22 percent, and they lived happily ever after.

The obvious fairy tale imagery above is just to make the point that classic storytelling is simple... and that business storytelling *must* be simple.

Simple case studies are a rock solid way to show your competence. For illustrating how a previous client succeeded because of your value-add, P.O.S.E. is a quick 'n dirty formula.

To make your story even more compelling, however, will take more time, more effort and a more powerful formula.

The Hero's Journey

Courage isn't the lack of fear. It's looking fear in the face and beating it. That's what heroes do. And that's what great characters and great brands do.

Heroes are not perfect. They simply don't do everything perfectly, and certainly not right from the start.

Lovers and customers won't care, and usually won't believe you, if you pound your chest with one success story after another in which you were perfect.

Do you want to capture their hearts? Show your vulnerability at one point in your life, your career, or your new startup.

"I found myself down and out, sleeping on a friend's pullout sofa. The only thing I could hope for was that this was rock bottom. And that's when I bumped into an old college friend who was down and out like me. It was in a coffee shop, where we first came up with the crazy idea…"

You won't be *anybody's* hero if you have always been riding high.

A true hero has been kicked in the teeth and dragged through the mud. She has slowly gotten back on her feet with a black eye and a bloody nose.

Then she begrudgingly saw the need to change and, with it, came an acute pang of fear as the little voice inside whispered, "I'm not able to accomplish what I know I really need to do."

Indeed, *struggle* is central to the journey, to the plot.

Heroes don't go from one success to another. That's why they're heroes, and that's why they're more successful in the long run.

If you like literature, or even mainstream movies, you've probably been sucked into *The Hero's Journey* without even knowing that the writers had a formula to their story.

Think Neo in *The Matrix*.

Think Luke Skywalker in *Star Wars*.

Think *Harry Potter*.

As William Bernhard writes in *Creating Character – Bringing Your Story To Life*, "The protagonist is only as interesting as the antagonist." To be clear, your story is only as interesting as your main character, and your main character is only as interesting as the challenge the antagonist presents him.

In love, your story's antagonist could be those little town blues, those big city challenges or that first career step that was just so wrong for you.

The important thing in heroic stories is that you (or your main character) did something about it, in spite of the many obstacles that had to be overcome (the plot), and that you learned something from it, which gives your story meaning (the theme, or moral of the story).

In business start-ups, the antagonist could be the cold, cruel marketplace that knocked you flat on your proverbial ass. Your plot could be built around you coming to the realization that a new product could be valuable in the marketplace. The path was not clear and the challenges were many, but those challenges helped you develop your product in a way that was even better for your customers than what you originally envisaged.

You can also build a good story about a customer's situation or challenge, and how you helped them. That could put you in the role of the mentor below. Just think! You could be the Professor Dumbledore in *Harry Potter*, Morpheus in *The Matrix*, or Obi-Wan Kenobi in *Star Wars*.

What kind of hardship did the antagonist cause you or your main character? If you know this, now you can craft your *Hero's Journey*.

One could take a literature course for an entire semester on The Hero's Journey. Here it is in abbreviated form.

Call To Adventure

- One day, you wake up, and you realize the world is cruel. If that's not bad enough news, you also realize that only you can save it.
- One night, Harry Potter realized that he was a wizard and that there was a dark force that would take over both the wizard and muggle worlds, bringing doom and gloom to all of humanity. Someone had to do extinguish the dark force, and apparently only Harry could.

Resistance To The Call

- You struggle coming to grips with the fact that it's really up to you, and only you, to save the world. Deep inside, you do believe it, but you use every type of rationalization to resist being called.
- Harry knew he was odd, but he couldn't quite believe he was a wizard and that an entire wizard world existed out there. But what he really didn't *want* to believe was that only he could save the world. Even if he *were* the only one, he didn't want to believe that he had the abilities, because this only put a bigger burden on him.

Crossing The Threshold

- You start to believe that you do have the power, that you could be the master of your own destiny. So you take the first steps. You're not convinced... yet... and you continue doubting, particularly because the journey quickly becomes tougher than you expected and the goal seems next to impossible to reach.

- Harry is now convinced that he's *the one*. He's ready for the long road ahead, but he also sees that this dark force is not only dark, but immensely powerful, with passionate supporters. Harry really questions his abilities because he knows it really matters.

The Belly Of The Whale

- You've invested your money in your startup and, even more worrisome, you've got other investors in it, too. You simply can't turn back.
- Harry sees the dark force as despicable. He also learns about how and why his parents died for him. He feels the powerful force of their love. The risk is high, but his love for his parents, his friends and the greater good is infinite. He commits to extinguishing the dark force, even if it means his own death.

Meeting The Mentor

- Paradoxically, while you're the only one who can vanquish the antagonist-enemy, you can't do it alone. "When the student is ready, the teacher appears." Your mentor is imperfect and flawed to the point that he or she may even have some skeletons in the closet. The mentor can't achieve your mission, due to lack of resources, creative abilities or other obligations. Again, only you can achieve the mission, yet you can only do it with the wisdom and support of your mentor.
- Harry meets Professor Dumbledore. Dumbledore knows why Harry is the chosen one. Dumbledore leads Harry slowly through a search of the head, heart and the forces of good and evil, because he also knows Harry is just a kid. Harry's got the heart, the soul

and the commitment, but he doesn't have the wisdom. Dumbledore lets Harry have a few failures, yet he is unrelenting in being there when there is a lesson to be learned. He doesn't provide all the answers; sometimes he provides only the questions. Later in the story, we realize that Dumbledore even went through a wicked, dark period, but he worked his way through it. Thus, he is even wiser.

The Road of Trials

- You don't get it right at first. That would simply be too easy with all of the challenges you went through to get this far, right? This is the heart of the plot, the conflict. You're in the thick of the shit, and the shit is *very* thick. But this struggle actually enables you to understand the marketplace and build an even better solution than you ever imagined.
- Harry has more antagonists than you can count on both hands. He has nuisances like the Malfoys. He has Professor Snape, who we don't know until the end whose side he's really on. He's got cats and rats and Dementors. He's got the irresistibly hateful Bellatrix Lestrange. And he's got The Dark Lord himself, Voldemort. Each of these antagonists brings Harry one trial after another. And this is what makes Harry such an interesting protagonist, and why JK Rowling sold a gazillion books.

The Ultimate Boon

- You finally get it right, and it's bigger and better than anything you ever expected, but you know it's only the beginning. You know the mission is to bring your valuable expertise to others, to be the missionary, the prophet, of your value proposition.
- Harry has it out with Voldemort. It's the ultimate battle, and it's not just physical, it's spiritual. It's good versus evil, darkness versus light, hate versus love. When it's over, when Harry vanquishes

The Dark Lord, the surviving haters know their battle is lost forever, and the light shines.

The Return Home & Master of Two Worlds

- Now, after achieving your mission, you're not only the master of
  that project, you have become the master of the everyday world,
  too. You know how to apply this to customer needs. Now you
  know how to help others, to touch the lives of those struggling.
  Your new goal is to spread the love.
- Years later, Harry lives an almost normal life in an almost normal
  suburb with an almost normal wife and family. The world is not
  just safe. The world is filled with love, because Harry and his loving supporters conquered darkness.

Theme / Essence

- Every time you communicate this to clients, or whenever you're
  out on a date or going deeper in a relationship, this is your one,
  big value-add. "And so, this is what we learned." This is the
  essence of your character and the compelling reason to work
  with you.
- Near the end of every *Harry Potter* book, JK Rowling includes
  a scene where the conversation turns to *love*. In *The Prisoner of
  Azkaban*, Harry's godfather, Sirius Black, engages Harry in a deep
  conversation about Harry's parents and the power of their love.
  In *The Deathly Hallows*, a few chapters before the ultimate show-
  down, Harry goes halfway to heaven and meets Professor Dumbledore. Dumbledore first tells Harry that he can choose the easy
  way and go with him back to heaven, but then the world will
  perish. Harry laments all those who have died. To which Dumbledore replies with the most quoted line in the series: "Don't pity
  the dead, Harry. Pity the living, and above all, pity those who live
  without love."

That's right, JK Rowling's theme is pervasive throughout. Over seven long books, she wrote 1,080,000 words... to say three:

Love conquers all.

Rowling does not waste a word. Every word either drives the plot or develops characters designed to reinforce this one big message, the theme.

OK, OK. You may not believe that Harry Potter is the greatest love story ever told, perhaps because you've read more than I have and, certainly you've read things that I haven't.

But one cannot deny the success of JK Rowling, and it's *not* because *Harry Potter* is mere entertainment about a few kids using magic wands to get out of high school mischief.

It's multi-dimensional, wonderful storytelling that has touched the hearts of millions. It goes deep into the human condition, the timeless and universal condition of human nature.

Harry takes on hatred, and he's surrounded by love.

His hateful foe at times seems invincible. Harry has more than his share of failures in his quest to conquer Voldemort. Yet his loving supporters, from his mother who died for him to his friends and quirky professors who support him in every step of his mission... they all love him.

Harry embodies love, and this is the theme.

Love conquers all.

So as you write your story, make every word count. Know *why* you're telling the story. What is the essence of your story?

Develop your plot, your struggles or the struggles of a customer with whom you've mentored to success.

Do this in as few words as possible – fewer, in fact, than the number of words in this, my longest chapter. But show a struggle. Make it heroic.

If you can turn your business stories into hero snippets, you will engage your buyers.

Look at Harry's story. Look at Neo's. Look at Luke's.

From the very beginning, their missions were overwhelming, seemingly impossible at times, and they failed more times than they succeeded.

And that's why we love them.

That's why we love great movies, great stories and, particularly, *The Hero's Journey*. We love these heroic characters because their challenges are bigger than our challenges and, so, they put our challenges in context.

That's why your customers will love you, too.

That's why your customers will feel you are capable of loving *them*!

You're not some self-absorbed, entitled banker whose daddy sent him through Yale, who now sits in his corner office and will trade in his Ferrari next year for a new one.

Not you!

You've spit blood while laying face down in the mud!

You've been vulnerable!

You've gotten back up and beaten the odds!

Don't talk just about your victories. Talk about how you were victorious *after* you faced your demons.

It's simply more engaging, compelling and loveable.

WOULD I LIE TO YOU?

Some salespeople dislike prospects who are a bit too tough and a bit too direct. Some even avoid them.

This is foolish.

Far worse than a straight-talking tough-guy is the nice guy… who lies!

Yet, we shouldn't demonize those who lie, either. They often have kind reasons for doing so.

When prospects lie, it's important for the salesperson to understand that they're not necessarily *trying* to be dishonest. Lying often says less about their ethics and more about their sensitivity. Not all buyers want to be mean. Many are simply trying to be nice. They're putting *nice* before *ethics.*

As silly as this may sound, they don't want to hurt your feelings!

Again, *Hitch, The Love Doctor* sets the record straight.

Hitch tells Albert, his client who has fallen in love with Allegra after a first encounter, "Of course she's going to lie to you. She's a nice person. What else is she going to say? She doesn't even know you yet!"

Dates lie to be nice. So do customers.

Don't be offended by a prospect's ethics in these situations. Be grateful for their sensitivity to your feelings.

But, at the same time, don't seek sensitivity. Be acutely aware of yet another paradox: cruelty is usually kinder. You don't want prospects to be nice to you if *nice* means giving you false expectations and sucking the life out of your time management and resource allocation.

Reality is king. Straight talk is golden.

If a prospect were to *cruelly* tell you there wasn't a chance in hell that you'll get their business, you could move on. You could spend your time and resources on more prospecting or developing the higher-probability deals in your pipeline.

And if a prospect is a bit tough yet says there is a chance, albeit a tiny one, you could explore what stands in your way. You could get to the heart of engagement. "Where do you see the biggest hurdle in moving forward?"

If the buyer is too nice, if the buyer is not cruel enough, if the buyer sugar-coats reality, you might not explore appropriately.

So don't take offense when a prospect lies to you, especially in the early stages of a sale. But don't take it at face value, either.

Appreciate the liar's sensitivity. Then take the responsibility to keep it safe and explore by prompting for concerns.

Why would I lie to you?

CHAPTER
26

YOU'RE NOT TALKING TO ME, BABY

Patrizia had divorced and, a year later, had finally picked herself up, dusted herself off and started dating.

After a few false starts, she met Jimmy at a friend's party, and sparks flew. The chemistry was instantaneous and it wasn't long before they were in an exclusive relationship.

The feelings grew quickly and deeply, and so did the sense of commitment. And that's when they hit the wall.

Jimmy suddenly got cold feet. Patrizia loved him too much to just let it go. She took him out for dinner and asked him what it was he wasn't sure of.

Jimmy didn't have kids and was now too old to really want them. He wasn't sure if he wanted a partner who did. Patrizia understood, but pointed out that her kids were in their teens, were relatively low-maintenance, and were getting more mature and independent every year.

Jimmy squirmed uncomfortably and admitted it was more about his independence. He didn't want to always take his partner along for weekends with his long-term friends, as he had taken Patrizia a few weekends earlier. Patrizia understood this, as well. She pointed out that she liked a certain amount of space herself, and that she certainly could accommodate her partner's need for space.

Then Jimmy said his mother was aging, and he needed time for her. Patrizia again understood... and realized that Jimmy wasn't being sincere.

Every time Patrizia tackled one objection, Jimmy came up with another.

This is the sign of *insincere objections.*

In a sale, insincere objections are often the most difficult to overcome... because they're not what's really bothering the buyer, and because they're vague. Dealing with insincere objections can be like trying to put a nail through a drop of water. The water keeps moving away.

The first task for the salesperson is to identify when an objection is sincere or insincere.

Sincere objections are clear, quantifiable and rational. When sincere objections are overcome, the sales process often proceeds constructively.

Insincere objections, on the other hand, can usually be identified as vague and difficult to quantify or pinpoint.

The prospect's reason for insincere objections are not rational, but emotional. The prospect is often hiding something, be it some personal insecurity or lack of transparency.

"I'm really not the decision-maker here, and I don't want you to think I'm a dweeb," is often the unspoken reason.

Or, "We're about to do a deal with your most direct competitor. We don't have the courage to look you in the eye and tell you this."

That's the reason. Here's the *real indicator* of insincere objections. They follow the pattern shown above between Patrizia and Jimmy. When one objection is sufficiently addressed, another one surfaces.

Sometimes insincere objections are insurmountable, but not always.

Over dessert, Patrizia reached across the table and took Jimmy's hand.

"I don't believe you," she said. "I don't believe a god damned word you're saying, Jimmy. But I love you… and I want to get to the bottom of this. What's really bothering you?"

When Jimmy paused, Patrizia knew there was some real reason that Jimmy didn't have the courage to tell her… until Patrizia made it safe for him, while also laying down the ultimatum.

"Do you want to throw this all away, Jimmy?" she asked. "Because I can't go on like this. I can if I know what it is I need to work on, or what you will commit to working on. Tell me what's going on in that heart of yours."

Jimmy opened the flood gates. "I'm struggling with my company, with my income, with my ability to take a woman of your lifestyle out to dinners like this!"

Patrizia held his hand tighter.

Jimmy kept the flood gates open. "You've got a great job. When your last employer let you go because of the cutbacks, you had headhunters and employers all over you. It took you a month to get your new job, and it's even better than your last one. Me? I'm struggling!"

Patrizia smiled. "That's it?"

"Yeah, that's it!" Jimmy snapped. "It's not just about my income. It's about my self-respect."

Patrizia smiled. "Well, you'll have to work on that self-respect issue, but I'll tell you one thing that should help you get started. I might have a steady income, but *you*? You have courage. Don't you think I can sense that your company isn't rolling in it yet?

"I've got all the respect in the world for you," she continued. "When I lost my last job, I had a choice to start something for myself or accept job offers. It was an easy decision. I don't have the courage to go out on my own. I don't think I could do what you're doing. Take that as respect, mister. And don't think for a minute that I'll let money get in our way. If you were a dead beat, I'd throw you under the bus for being a dead beat. But you're not a dead beat. You're courageous and you're working hard. I've got all the respect in the world for you. And I'm paying the check tonight. You can cook for me on Saturday… unless you want to go away with your friends."

Jimmy laughed… and let a few tears drop. "I don't have the money to go away this weekend. But that's not my reason for wanting to be with you this weekend. How does Thai curry sound for Saturday?"

"I'll bring dessert." Patrizia had her shoe off and rubbed her foot inside Jimmy's leg. "And it will be spicier than your Thai curry!"

Don't let insincere objections get in your way. Have the courage to engage and respectfully dig deeper. If your respectful digging upsets the customer, then you probably weren't going to get a deal anyway.

If, on the other hand, the customer feels your love and tells you the truth, you'll earn a lot of respect, and maybe you'll earn a deal.

27

MAKE LOVE, NOT WAR

Most marriage counselors deal with conflict resolution on a regular basis. Yet most also say the vast majority of conflicts are avoidable in the first place.

Sure, it takes two to tango, but we can only control our own selves, and even that is a challenge. Here again, it begins with emotions, but this time, they're not our customer's or of love interest's emotions, they're *our* emotions.

Emotionally, we're programmed not for the kitchen but for the cave. Mentally, we're programmed to survive more than to behave compatibly.

So the modern-day caveman and cavewoman scenario goes like this. Something our partner says triggers a defense mechanism. We react without consciously thinking about it.

Our emotional-mental cocktail causes us to draw a conclusion that often paints our partner as being on the attack. We draw an immediate conclusion and create our own story that our partner has acted out of ill will.

Physically, our breathing becomes shallow and rapid, our pulse quickens, our focus narrows.

Bang! We say something defensive, which is perceived by our partner as actually being offensive. Our partner's defensive emotions are, in turn, triggered, and, *oops, you did it again.*

And. It. Escalates.

Maybe it's our partner's fault, or maybe, *just maybe*, it's we who have seen the storm in a teacup.

The difference between a spouse and a prospect, however, is that you're hitched to the spouse until death or divorce do you part. You're only hitched to the prospect until rejection does you not a phone call returneth.

Take a step back. The future is more important than the past. The conflict could have well been avoided had *the objection been handled effectively.*

Perhaps the romantic partner needed clarification on something and merely inquired. With proper handling of the inquiry, the relationship is not only preserved, it's strengthened. But if your habits are that of the caveman or cavewoman more than those of the modern man or woman, you can find yourself out in the dog house pretty fast.

In a business sense, objections are most often demonstrations of buyer interest. The buyer needs the salesperson to help her work through a perceived problem. If this is handled well, you could be well on your way toward deal closure.

You think this happens more in the marital kitchen than it does in the customer meeting room?

Imagine this scene. An event marketing sales agent named Jeffrey was representing a major sports event, a World Championship, in the area of sponsorship sales. He secured a meeting with KP, the Worldwide Head of Advertising & Sponsorship of an Asian consumer electronics company.

Jeffrey informed the sports event's Marketing Director, Raoul, about the upcoming meeting, and Raoul insisted on joining the meeting, as was his contractual right.

At the meeting, Jeffrey and Raoul presented KP with the sponsorship opportunity, the core values of the sport and a business case as to how the consumer electronics brand could benefit from such a sponsorship.

KP seemed genuinely interested. He agreed that an event of this type could complement his brand's portfolio.

As could be expected in a first meeting, KP had some concerns that needed to be addressed.

"I really was not aware that your sport had a year-round schedule of competitions," KP said. "It makes sense, but to be honest, I'm only aware of your sport during the Olympic Games."

Jeffrey, the agent, replied, "It's not the first time we've heard that, KP, and I think we can address your concerns. Is there anything specific we should cover?"

"Well, I guess my lack of awareness," KP said, "is linked to never seeing your sport on TV, except during the Games. I don't want to bring my company into a sponsorship that has no TV visibility."

Jeffrey was about to empathize with KP by agreeing that the lack of TV is a reasonable perception, and then show KP a chart of TV distribution and audience figures around the world.

But before Jeffrey could do so, Raoul, the event Marketing Director, yelped, "Not on TV? No way! We've got *great* broadcast coverage!"

Raoul then proceeded to slide an event fact book across the table, with his arms and large upper body following the tome.

"Look at these numbers!" Raoul insisted. "We've got ESPN in the US with some events in prime time. In Western Europe, we're on most of the mainstream broadcasters, and where we're not, we're on Eurosport. Australia, mostly prime time. No, no! You're wrong. We've got great coverage!"

Jeffrey tried to rein Raoul in, but Raoul still didn't feel his point was clear. His caveman emotions still hadn't driven enough nails in the coffin.

So he used a sledgehammer to drive the last stake right in to KP's heart. "I can't believe it when I hear people in this industry say we don't have television!"

KP pulled back and nodded, "I guess you're right."

But the damage had been done.

Jeffrey tried to reel it all back in. He said, "Raoul, given that KP is based in Asia-Pacific, I can really see his point-of-view here. In fact, if I were in your shoes, KP, I'd probably say the same thing.

"Now, we are talking with NHK Broadcasting in Japan and SBS in South Korea nearly every week," Jeffrey said, "and I think we'll have a breakthrough there in the next month or two. We can keep you up to date on that, on a confidential basis, of course."

"Please do," KP said politely.

"You're absolutely right, KP," Jeffrey continued. "The World Championships, not to mention the full seasonal calendar, have had an inconsistent history. Even today, in markets like Asia Pacific, we've got work to do, and we're on it, as we mentioned in Japan and South Korea. Western Europe and North America are very strong, as Raoul points out. And if we can deliver similar coverage in Asia Pacific in the next three months, with specific measurables and answers to your earlier questions, how do you see it?"

KP said, "It's a great opportunity."

For the rest of the meeting, KP never said more than one sentence, and none of them were more than a half-dozen words.

KP would not commit to a specific date for a follow-up meeting and, when prompted, just said, "Update me as you make progress."

Jeffrey called KP the next day to thank him for the meeting and to review next steps. KP took Jeffrey's call. Since he had a six-year relationship with Jeffrey, KP was clear but polite, and said his brand had other priorities. They would not sponsor the World Championships.

Jeffrey probed for specifics.

"We think the fit is good," KP said, "but we buy relationships. We're just not comfortable. Of course I'll be happy to work with you personally on other projects when you see a fit."

Jeffrey was glad that his relationship with KP was seemingly preserved, but he couldn't help but see the lose-lose-lose. Jeffrey lost a high-probability commission. KP lost a great sponsorship opportunity for his brand. And Raoul lost two million euros for the World Championship organizers.

It's not hard to see that the turning point in the potential sale occurred when Raoul, the event Marketing Director, behaved as though he was *disagreeing* with KP, merely in response to KP's legitimate concern – a concern which, if handled well, could have led to a strong bond.

The problem is, it was hard for Raoul to see.

Clearly, it was incumbent upon Jeffrey and Raoul to counter KP's objection by showing *data* that the TV numbers were good and getting better. But Raoul's *tone* was one of disagreement, not that of constructively… and lovingly… addressing a concern.

Any marriage counselor will tell you that a pattern of snap judgments and quick, win-lose retorts can be fatal in a marriage. It can be fatal in a sale, too.

You're not there to win a battle. Battles in sales may not lead to wars, but they do lead to rejections.

If there is *one thing* that any salesperson should do when a buyer raises a concern, it's to *agree* with the buyer's reason for stating the objection.

This does not mean that you agree with the content of the objection. It does not mean that you roll over and play dead to keep the buyer happy.

It means that you build a bond, an alliance, with the buyer by first affirming that they are acting responsibly by voicing their objection.

"If I were in your shoes, I'd probably say the same thing."

Then you show them the data or information that wins the point. Your *content* has to trump their question, no doubt, but your *tone* should be one of winning their hearts – not of disagreeing, but rather, of agreeing.

If the buyer remains silent, it's fair to say, "Did that address your question?" or, "Is there anything else in this area that you'd like us to clarify?"

Or, "Honey, I know why you feel this way."

When it comes to handling objections, make love, not war.

28

A GENTLEMAN IS A PATIENT WOLF

The politically correct are going to cry "*Incorrect!*" on this one.

Here goes.

It's as natural for a man to want a woman as it is for a wolf to want prey.

Modern women may ask a man for his phone number or even make a first date, just like marketing may attract a customer to seek out a vendor. But once the game is on, a man who does not show enough interest through appropriate action will more often than not lose the woman's interest.

Call me a traditionalist or call me a sexist, but, in essence, a man is a wolf.

A *gentle*-man, however, is polite. He's charming. He pushes the romantic process forward, but he's not *too* pushy, either.

He's a patient wolf.

The *patient wolf* quote comes from a woman, by the way, and we can give her the benefit of any doubt and assume she was a lady, too – 1950's American film star, Lana Turner.

A gentleman wants something, yet he defers to the lady. Whether she wants meaningful romance or a steamy romp, he has the confidence to believe he can woo her, and he has the charm to make her feel good about the process.

The gentleman makes sure that, whatever the outcome, it won't endanger the lady physically, nor will it jeopardize her reputation socially. The gentleman takes the responsibility for moving the relationship forward, albeit with confidence and patience.

W. Anton's bold and edgy book, *The Manual: What Women Want And How To Give It To Them*, is built on three pillars: confidence, charm and responsibility, as mentioned earlier.

A patient wolf can be defined in the context of all three pillars. With respect to the third, when a man is in pursuit of a woman, it's his responsibility to push the process forward.

A woman often wants to proceed with romance and intimate relations, but whether through genetic programming or social conditioning, she has built-in obstacles that most men either physically don't have for themselves or socially don't worry about.

Nevertheless, most available women *do* want the men they find worthy to court them.

Due to genetic programming, most women are simply more cautious than men when it comes to engaging in sex and committing to relationships.

To ensure survival of the species, a woman's genetic job is to produce healthy children and nurture them. She will, therefore, inherently take the necessary steps to ensure that her body and her children's bodies will not be harmed. The perceived risk factor needs to be low, lest a woman will go into caution mode and default to *just say no*.

Due to social conditioning, a woman will want to be a lady or, at very least, be *seen* as a lady. She has a reputation to keep, so she doesn't want to be seen as too eager, too easy or too promiscuous. Beyond her reputation, she also has her own self-esteem to live with.

So through the ages, the woman will make the man *work for it.* As the physical risk factor needs to be low for the woman to say "yes," so it goes, the social trust factor needs to be high. A gentleman has to mitigate these risks and build trust in order to motivate the lady to move forward.

Likewise, most *customers* will make a *salesperson* work for it, even if the customer is attracted to the salesperson, even if the customer desires the potential solution from the very beginning.

Due to negotiation-type leveraging, customers usually don't want to appear too eager, too easy or, we can say, too promiscuous. They want their vendors to work for it, even those vendors that are seen to be suitable early on. Often, customers *are* interested in proceeding toward a solution and a deal, yet they *welcome* the salesperson taking the effort and responsibility to push things forward – in a gentlemanly way, of course.

Due to internal, organizational dynamics, customers don't want to take risks that are perceived to be too high by their managers and peers. They have their individual reputations to protect, and selecting an unsuitable vendor could jeopardize this. Make no mistake, selecting the wrong vendor can cost a manager her job!

So a salesperson has to mitigate these risks in order to motivate even the most motivated prospects to move forward.

Being too pushy can kill buyer trust, yet being too distant or aloof can create buyer skepticism.

Ergo, to win a customer's heart, the successful salesperson must take the responsibility to drive the relationship forward, yet also be a patient wolf.

Only gentlemen – and ladies – need apply.

CHAPTER

29

↓

KISS HER ON THE FIRST DATE

Some sales managers become baffled by the salesperson who is knowledgeable, personable, trustworthy – and who gets many first meetings yet rarely closes deals.

What's even more frustrating, not to mention even more resource-depleting, is the salesperson who meets regularly with repeat prospects, but rarely comes away with any *advances*, being firm next steps in which the prospect puts *skin in the game*.

If the sales manager were to go out with the salesperson to observe and improve skills, she might discover that the salesperson is too *nice*. Some salespeople are more comfortable building friendly relationships than they are professionally developing a sale.

As lovers, these salespeople would essentially be falling into the *friend zone*. They're not even trying to kiss their prospects on the proverbial lips on the first date. To them, a kiss on the first date would be too risky, so they hold meeting after meeting building comfortable, friendly relationships.

Yep, they settle into the friend zone… and often get nowhere.

To hell with *the friend zone*!

If a prospect likes to buy you lunch (on their expense account) and pick your brain, but doesn't engage in a long-term solution or even an initial transaction, why spend your time giving them information and becoming their friend? Why not qualify these prospects in a gentlemanly way and, when qualified negatively, professionally decline the next free lunch and spend your energy elsewhere?

If the apple of your eye wants a compassionate ear for his life challenges but doesn't want *action*, why spend your time becoming his friend, when what you really want is a lover? Why not look under other apple trees?

Through a consulting project a decade ago, I became good friends with Ferdinand. Because the project was in London, a city that was home to neither him nor me, we often worked late and walked back to the hotel together. This led to frequent dinners or drinks where we really got to know each other.

Ferdinand was fit, funny and had a great smile. He was easily approach-able, and had little problems starting conversations.

He'd occasionally leave parties and happy hours with phone numbers of attractive women. He'd meet them for coffee, then a glass of wine, then a movie, then dinner, then walks in the park, all the while listening and sharing life stories and relationship stories, and then…

… it would be too late. Ferdinand would fall into the friend zone.

After so many friendly dates, Ferdinand would occasionally muster up the courage to go for a kiss or, worse yet, suggest the idea of a romantic relationship.

The woman would be surprised and invariably reject his intentions of romance. They would stay friends, but even the friendship waned sooner or later.

This rejection would only make it more difficult for Ferdinand to muster up the early courage in future dates with other women, and history would repeat itself. He'd fall into the friend zone again.

It was a vicious cycle.

Ferdinand and I stayed in touch over the next decade with birthday wishes, New Year's greetings, not to mention Facebook posts. We would have the occasional drink when he was in my town or I in his.

Then, I noticed on Facebook that Ferdinand's luck seemed to be changing.

Many of his posts were photos of him out partying, often with very attractive women. There was something about the photos that indicated these women were in Ferdinand's *hot zone*. Physically, they were very close to him – like, *all over him* – and, they seemed to be enjoying themselves as much as he was.

If this was the friend zone, man, was it spicy! And I was curious.

As luck would have it, I had a meeting in his city a few months later, so we arranged dinner. Before the waiter had even taken our order, I asked him if there was a lady in his life.

"A lady?" he smiled, a bit mischievously, "As in *one*?"

"Man," I replied, "I don't want to pry, but I need a little more info."

"Pry all you want, man. I'm happy to report that life is great," he started. "Over the past couple of years, I've gotten really comfortable with the whole dating thing. I've met some awesome women. I'm still looking for the love of my life, but I'm not desperate for company, if that's what you mean."

"Yeah?" I grinned. "Man, I can't tell you how happy that makes me, because when we worked on the London project, I have to say, I was worried about you. I could sense your desperation. Some people thought you were gay and had not come out. You know I wouldn't have a problem with that. I was just sensing you were straight and simply in a romantic rut."

"*Rut?*" Ferdinand laughed. "Man, I was in a *crevasse*. I was dying for sex. I was dying for a relationship, and I really didn't know what to do."

"So what *did* you do?" I asked. "It looks like you're lighting the world on fire on Facebook, and now you're telling me you're thrashing half of Western Europe. What's changed?"

"Thrashing half of Western Europe is an exaggeration, although I appreciate your views on Brand Ferdinand," he said. "What happened? A few things, actually, but I can honestly say, one thing made a huge difference. Going for the kiss."

"Ha!" I laughed, happy for my friend. "So, you meet a woman somewhere, you make a date, and after the date, as you're saying good night, you go for the kiss?"

"Man, you're old fashioned," he laughed. "I often go for the kiss right after meeting her."

"Really? Oh man, you're a star!"

"I had a great relationship with Jody before she went back to San Francisco," Ferdinand said. "I hope she comes back. She really could be the one. Anyway, Jody and I met at a party and the chemistry was great. When she said good night, I told her I'd I walk her to the bus stop. I didn't wait for the bus to come. I kissed her 100 meters before the bus stop. I was nervous, but the moment we started kissing, I knew she had been hoping I would. She kept kissing me, and when the bus came, she laughed and said, 'You're not coming home with me… but I can wait for the next bus.'"

"You da' man!" I grinned some more.

"Oh, it's not all success. One woman pulled back as I started to kiss her. She got a pissed off look on her face and said, 'What's *that* all about?' But at least I knew. I mean, I didn't hurt her. I just tried to kiss her. She got pissed off. That's her problem. My problem was solved," Ferdinand laughed. "At least I knew where we stood."

"I guess you could say you're qualifying your prospects early," I joked. "Do they often get pissed off?"

"No," he said. "Some let me know they're not interested in anything romantic, but you know what? Women like to know that you find them attractive."

"So you're not wasting your time on poor leads," I laughed, "and you're making the female population happy in the process."

"Exactly," he said. "And sometimes I'm making *myself* happy in the process. There might be a moment of surprise, but when she smiles and stares at my lips…"

"And so you know," I said.

"And so I avoid the friend zone. Don't get me wrong. I have my share of women friends, but at least it's my choice as much as hers," Ferdinand said. "But, really, if I want romance with a woman I meet, well, I go for the kiss early. That way I'm not wasting her time *or* mine."

"It's not like they hate you afterwards, either," I said.

"Usually it's just the opposite," he said. "They usually like you more. I'm convinced that it's easier to go for romance early, and then fall back to the friend zone with a really great vibe, than it is to fall into the friend zone and try to move it to the romance zone."

To the women reading this and shrieking for political correctness, come on! You have your ways of initiating a first kiss, too.

It could be a smile with the occasional glance down at a man's lips.

Or it could be as *Hitch, The Love Doctor* said. "A woman that doesn't want to be kissed puts her key in the door and opens it. A woman that wants to be kissed fiddles with her keys."

Either way, here is a behavioral truth regarding modern relationships. It's easier to go from the romance zone to the friend zone than it is to go the other way. The fact is, we respect people who nudge us… who go for the kiss with us.

Customers respect this, too. They actually see it as confident and professional.

Salespeople need to be clear up front. You're not there to waste the customer's time… *or your own!*

If you qualify a customer, if you ask for an advance and don't get it, but then a few months later the customer calls you back, you're in a good position to go in and talk about a real need that they want to dedicate resources and budget towards. Or perhaps they might want to refer you to someone. They might set you up with a blind date. After all, they see you as professional, and everyone likes to refer true professionals.

This happens more often to the salesperson who is clear in his intentions early, who goes for the proverbial kiss on the first date, than it does to the salesperson who falls into the friend zone.

If, as a salesperson, you don't tactfully make your intentions known up front, albeit while showing value, some prospects will squeeze you dry.

They will meet with you, then go quiet for months. Then they'll call you with "something that's developing fast." They'll invite you to lunch, pick your brain again and say, "Let's talk next week."

Then they go quiet again.

Sound familiar?

All too often, these friend zone prospects have no intention of hiring you, but they reap benefit from your free expertise, or maybe they simply get the pleasure of your company, the pleasure of you as an easy date during an otherwise open lunch hour.

Much like a date, they have no intention of sleeping with you, let alone falling in love with you, but they do have the proverbial evening free and don't want to be lonely.

Customers respect salespeople who are clear and confident. Go for the advance. Ask the customer to put skin in the game. Qualify them, and don't be shy about it.

Go for the proverbial kiss.

If they're not ready to sleep with you, they will still respect you. They might even become friends with you, and they might even refer you.

After all, if you're going to be friends, you might as well be friends with benefits.

↓

CHAPTER 30

SKIN IN THE GAME &
THE ART OF THE NEXT STEP

Another friend of mine had been dating a divorced mother for several months.

Everything seemed to be going well, but he wanted more commitment. While it felt mutual, he really wasn't certain what *she* wanted, especially in view of her family responsibilities.

One evening over a romantic dinner, he opened a conversation about her kids and how they would see their mom with a committed boyfriend.

She smiled. She felt the years since the separation were enough, and that the kids would probably even welcome their mom having a partner.

So he suggested they find a way for the kids to meet him.

She laughed excitedly. "I have the kids this weekend. Why don't you come over Saturday for an early dinner with us?"

My friend had earned his girlfriend's trust, and she was motivated to invest heavily in the next step. She was putting *skin in the game*.

So often, salespeople leave a first meeting with a new prospect feeling optimistic. "They walked us to the elevator, patted my project manager and me on the backs, and said, 'We like this a lot!'"

While words like "Send us a proposal" may lift your spirits, that could turn out to be like meeting someone at a bar who says, "Sure, give me a call," but then never agreeing to a date… no skin in the game… no investment in the next steps.

When you leave a first meeting, what will your *prospect* do to contribute to such next steps?

Is the prospect putting skin in the game? Or is the prospect sitting on the sidelines by asking you to do a lot of follow-up work, with no commitment on his part?

If the prospect is simply going to wait for you to develop something, it doesn't mean that a deal is dead, but it's not a great sign, either.

Customers are usually polite in that they don't want to hurt your feelings face-to-face, and sometimes they're simply not focused enough to solve the problem that's right in your sweet spot.

All too often, after you send your key findings or, even worse, a full proposal, the prospect goes quiet. "I'll be travelling. I'll get back to you in a couple of weeks."

And then you're in *chase* mode.

Sound familiar?

So how do you determine success in a first meeting, and how can you keep the prospect actively engaged?

How do you gauge the prospect's real interest, and how do you determine which opportunities among your active prospects to dedicate more of your time to?

It's called an *advance*.

The extent to which the prospect contributes to the next steps determines the quality of the advance. The extent to which the prospect dedicates resources to the next steps is a clear and strong indicator as to how motivated the prospect is to really work toward a deal.

Let's say Prospect A tells you at the end of a meeting, "Send me key findings and recommendations by the end of next week," while not really being clear as to what she'll do when she receives the findings.

And let's say Prospect B agrees, at various stages of a meeting, to set up a phone call between you and his Project Head, and to bring in three different people for a meeting next month, while also asking you, "Send me key findings and recommendations by the end of next week."

Which meeting do you gauge to be more successful?

Prospect B, because they have *advanced*. They are investing their resources in the next steps. They are putting skin in the game.

On which prospect's key findings and recommendations should you work more diligently?

Prospect B, of course.

Now, an advance is not only an indicator, a gauge, of a prospect's motivation. It can also be a *tactical tool* for ensuring – or at very least, encouraging – that an interested prospect stay engaged in that often difficult and uncertain period following a first or second meeting.

You can – and should – work *possible advances* into your meeting plan for each and every prospect visit, including upselling existing clients.

In your plan, define a successful meeting outcome by how the prospect might contribute to the next steps, and work these possible next steps in to your meeting objectives. You don't have to wait until the end of the meeting to ask for these advances. Sometimes it's simply more natural to ask for them if things are going well *in the middle* of the meeting.

And *sometimes,* prospects will offer advances as a natural part of the meeting. Take note of these advances and review them at the end of the meeting.

If the prospect does not agree to any specific advances, it is entirely within your right to ask for one, especially if you have work to do as a result of this meeting.

You have every right to say, "We'll be happy to prepare our key findings and recommendations, John, and send them at the end of the week. Could we arrange a meeting the following week with you and your IT infrastructure team?"

By having your desired advances planned before the meeting, you can quickly suggest them, or even adjust to a new advance based on new material you've discovered about the prospect during the meeting.

My friend asked his girlfriend for an advance, and she accepted by arranging dinner with her kids.

After that dinner, with the kids in bed and the two of them snuggling on the sofa, she offered another advance. "Why don't you and I drive to my parents' place next weekend?"

31

↓

PICK UP WHERE YOU LEFT OFF

Ronny and Alyssa met at a mutual friend's party and, three evenings later, had a great first date.

They met at a restaurant for a light dinner. They found some mutual interests, laughed a lot and, when they walked to Alyssa's car, they kissed… and kissed…

They agreed to meet the coming weekend, although they didn't have a firm plan. So when Ronny followed up, he suggested dinner at a trendy wine bar.

Alyssa arrived a few minutes after Ronny, who was sitting at a high-top table in front of two glasses of Sauvignon Blanc, Alyssa's favorite. She gave Ronny a hug and pressed her cheek against his, almost kissing, as she sat down.

They chatted the entire dinner… with this thing between them called *a table*.

When the check came, Ronny suggested they walk to a bar holding an open mike night, a few blocks a way.

As they walked, Ronny wanted to hold Alyssa's hand, but he wasn't sure. Alyssa wanted him to hold her hand, but didn't want to take his. In fact, she was dying to kiss Ronny... *really* kiss... like they had against her car a few nights earlier.

Once in the club, there were no free tables. Fortunately, Ronny recognized a few people at a table with an empty chair, and they found another chair nearby and pulled it up.

Introductions were made and the group conversation was good, but the connection between Ronny and Alyssa was becoming awkward.

The live music started, and the conversation only became more difficult. Ronny wondered if Alyssa was enjoying the date and, so it goes, Alyssa wondered if Ronny was enjoying the date.

They stayed until the end of the gig, and walked back to Alyssa's car, and kissed... but Ronny felt funny. And so did Alyssa.

Alyssa asked, "So, shall we see each other again?"

Ronny replied, "Well, yeah. I mean, if you want to. Do you want to have dinner next week?"

Alyssa agreed... but she drove home, doubting. When Ronny called her a few days later, Alyssa said she'd be busy that week, and that she'd confirm another date soon.

She never did.

Ronny had lost Alyssa's heart.

An online PR agency once pitched a major consumer goods company. In the first meeting, they really connected with the PR and social media managers.

The agency sparked interest with a crisp, short presentation and also asked good questions. They learned a lot about the company's challenges with their consumers and sales channels.

They agreed to meet a week later when Jackie, the Head of Marketing could attend.

"We would like you to show Jackie exactly what you showed us today," the PR manager said. "She'll love it."

No sooner had the agency left that first meeting and got in the cab than they said, "We're crazy if we show Jackie the exact same thing. That's like taking a step backwards."

So they decided to pick up where they had left off, not where they had started. They showed up a week later and kissed Jackie on the lips, so to say.

They began the second date, um, the second meeting, with brief findings from the first meeting, and added further insights and a more precise vision of a way forward.

The agency knew that the advertising and online managers would have given Jackie an overview from the first meeting, anyway, so they moved forward from there.

Not only did Jackie like it, so did the advertising and social media managers. The agency exceeded everyone's expectations on the customer side. They were winning their hearts.

Everyone was feeling that the initial attraction was moving toward a meaningful relationship. All it took was one more meeting, and they were sleeping together. They had a deal.

This is what Ronny and Alyssa, at the start of their second date, did *not* do. Instead of picking up where they had left off after the first date and moving forward, they took a step backwards and started all over again. It was awkward, so the fire went out almost as quickly as it started.

Either one of them, Ronny or Alyssa, could have picked up on the second date where they had left off on the first one.

Either one of them could have planted a wicked kiss on the other's lips at the wine bar.

Either one of them could have grabbed the hand of the other as they left the wine bar and walked to the gig.

Ronny could have planned the date differently from the start and, in fact, Alyssa could have suggested something different when Ronny proposed meeting at the wine bar for another dinner with another table between them.

Imagine if, at the start of the date, Ronny would have picked up Alyssa at her place. Imagine if either one of them had taken the initiative to pick up where they had left off, with a wicked kiss, some good ol' embracing and, "Oh, wow! I've really been looking forward to this."

But instead, they looked at the menu and ordered bruschetta.

Don't go backwards with your customer engagements.

Pick up where you left off, and go forward.

Don't meet expectations. Exceed them.

Keep stoking the fire, go forward and win their hearts.

CHAPTER
32

FALSE ASSUMPTIONS & SHUTTING UP

"I'm in love with you," Dovi, played by Liev Schreiber, said to his love interest, Avigal, played by Vanessa Paradis in the 2013 film, *Fading Gigolo*.

Avigail stayed quiet. So Dovi continued.

"I got jealous. It's hard for a man to understand a woman, what goes on, the feelings. I know, I know. I'm boring. But if a man can't get a woman out of his guts, if he can't get her out of his heart, that means something. Right?"

And, again, Dovi continued. "I'm in love with you, ok? Right? I know, I know. Maybe you don't love me, but…"

"Just be quiet," Avigail finally interrupted him. "I never said I didn't love you."

Dovi had won Avigail's heart, but he assumed he was crashing and burning.

Lovers do what Dovi did all the time. They make false assumptions, and they keep talking.

Salespeople do this all too often, too.

Don't assume customers don't love your stuff. Don't assume they don't love you. Don't assume you're not winning their hearts.

Don't make false, negative assumptions and feed them to the customer.

Indeed, sometimes you need to explore.

But sometimes, you need to shut up.

CHAPTER

33

ASK FOR THE "NO"

I had the joy of working in the 90's with Rob Prazmark, Olympic sponsorship salesman extraordinaire. We had pitched a $40 million Worldwide Olympic sponsorship to a major brand.

This was not a renewal with an incumbent sponsor of the likes of Coca-Cola or Visa. This was a big proposal to a prospective new sponsor, and this company had never sponsored anything nearly so expensive or resource-hungry.

We had met with the company's Chief Marketing Officer and his team on numerous occasions. At first, there was a lot of excitement within the entire marketing department. We clearly had seduced and engaged them.

As time marched on, however, the communication with the CMO and his team was becoming more and more vague, and less and less frequent. Somehow, we weren't winning their hearts.

Given that sponsorships of this size are so high profile and, let's not forget, so expensive, product category exclusivity is part of the game.

So as time marched on, so did our chances of selling the product category to another brand for the coming Games, even though the category was generally a hot one for sports event sponsorship.

When George and Irma met, sparks flew.

George's friends often told him it was a match made in heaven, and the first three months were not only exciting, but also easy and fun for both of them.

George had finalized his divorce about two years earlier. Irma had announced her separation from her emotionally abusive husband about six months prior to meeting George. As she was finalizing a lease for her own apartment, she and George decided it would be better to move in together.

To celebrate, they started looking in to flights to Marrakesh, and that's when things got gnarly.

Irma's husband suddenly told her he wanted to make it work, and he pressured her to stay. Irma became confused, so she moved in with her mother a half-hour away.

This made George's communication with Irma even more difficult, because it also coincided with her going quiet.

Was it her ex-husband's renewed declaration of love? Was it her genuine need to talk with her mother? Was it simply her confusion?

George didn't know. He probed, but when Irma wasn't quiet, she was unclear and evasive, even though she insisted that she was madly in love with George.

At first, George was satisfied with Irma's words. But as time marched on, he became uncomfortable with her actions. Whenever George would ask for clarity, she would ramble on. Whenever he asked her for a decision, she would justify why it was difficult.

So, George asked her for the *no*.

"I know it's difficult, Irma, but I'm struggling here, too," he said. "It will hurt me to break up, but *this* is killing me. So, I ask you. Are we going forward together, or are you going backward alone?"

Irma hesitated and justified.

So George said, "I need to know if you want to go forward with me. I need a *yes*. Anything that is not a simple and clear *yes* means *no*. So, is it *no?*"

"No," Irma said as she teared up. "I mean, it is *not a no*."

So George said, "Is that a *yes*? Are you going to move in with me?"

"Yes," Irma said, as she started crying. "I want to stay with my mom for a few weeks, just to ease the transition. I'll stay with you a few nights between now and then, and I'll move in at the beginning of the month. *Yes!*"

They both cried. Two nights later, they cancelled the trip to Marrakesh, but they made plans to go forward together.

On the Olympic sponsorship, Rob also asked the CMO for a *no*.

The infrequent and unclear communication had put us in an awkward position, so Rob called the CMO on a Monday morning. The CMO's assistant told Rob that the CMO was in a meeting, so Rob said, "Please tell him it's urgent and that I'm on hold."

When the CMO came on the line a minute later, Rob said, "Sorry for startling you, but this really is critical. I have a duty to my client, the IOC. I have to report to them that we are either going forward with you or we are not. If the latter, we will free up the product category and open discussions with your competitors. I have a meeting in Lausanne on Thursday. So, if I don't hear back from you by Wednesday, I will update the IOC that you are out. We will take it as a *no*. I fly out Wednesday night."

The CMO said, "Rob, I promise you an answer by Wednesday afternoon."

That same Monday morning, a mere two hours later, the CMO called Rob back and said, "Rob, I don't know where in the world you're planning to be on the afternoon of the 17th, but you'd better cancel it. I just got you 30 minutes with our CEO."

Rob replied, "Off the top of my head, I don't where I was planning to be on the 17th, either, but you can confirm it. I'll be there."

A few days after the CEO meeting, we had a signed Letter of Intent. And three months after that, we had a signed deal: 40 million bucks and a great new addition to our sponsorship program.

The sad truth is, people like options. Be they prospects or love interests, people like options. Options are luxuries. They allow the other party to reap certain benefits without consequences, without putting skin in the game.

The CMO wanted the Olympic sponsorship, but he had other worries, too. So why push the CEO for a $40 million commitment this month? No decision was an easy decision.

Once the CMO was faced with the sponsorship opportunity vanishing into thin air, however, the consequences became clear. A competitor might grab the sponsorship, and the CMO would have some explaining to do.

Likewise, Irma loved George, but she was too confused, so she froze. No decision was an easy decision.

As salespeople, we must never lose sight of the fact that our competitor is sometimes not just another company offering services similar to ours. Very often, our biggest competitor is no decision at all.

Does it hurt any more if you lose a deal to a direct competitor or to human inaction?

Does it hurt any more if you lose the love of your life to the ex-spouse, to another lover or to no one at all?

This is very different than assuming you're crashing and burning, as Dovi did above with Avigail. This is clarifying where your love interest stands, where your customer wants to go.

Certainly, you shouldn't go on a first date and ask for a *no*. Nor would you go into a first pitch and ask for one.

But when things get stuck and the apple of your eye prospect falls into non-decision mode, asking for the *no* is often your best course of action. If you get a *no*, you can move forward and concentrate on other prospects in the marketplace; you can move forward with your life!

But you may very well get a *yes.*

By asking for the *no*, you often get a *yes.*

↓

UNTIL YOU'RE GOING STEADY, YOU'RE NOT GOING STEADY

A global promotion agency once formed a joint venture with a smaller event management firm, and the relationship was consummated with both firms moving into a new office together.

At one of the first monthly management meetings, a Senior Vice President from the promotion side gave an update.

"It looks like we'll be consulting for (a prominent motor racing team)."

"Cool!" marveled one of the managers from the event team.

"What will we be doing for them?" another event guy asked.

"Well," the Sr. VP began, "We'll be looking at their sponsorships and branding. We'll be looking at developing some promos on ESPN. This could be a bridge into the Series, too, so it could lead to some event management business."

The optimism was sustained for the rest of the meeting, but not much beyond that.

That meeting was, in fact, the last time a clear update about the racing team was brought up, aside from occasional questions and vague answers.

The fact is, the racing team had asked for a small study about female fans in motor racing, which already existed in the firm's library. It was delivered on short timelines and at a cheap price. In the week following, the promotion agency went beyond the brief and delivered a freebie in the form of on-site hospitality recommendations.

There was never another formal meeting with the team. Indeed, there were impromptu greetings around the pits and VIP areas at races, and there were coffees at sports congresses. But the agency and the team had hardly had anything more than a one-night stand.

Meanwhile, the promo agency's Sr. VP reported, hoped and probably *believed* they were going steady.

Until you're going steady, you're not going steady!

One morning, I was having coffee with Phillip, an acquaintance in Zurich. He was telling me about his online dating experiences, and his dating overall.

He had split up with his long-term girlfriend a year earlier and, after a few months, had dusted himself off and was back out in the dating market. He was getting dates on a satisfactory basis, but they often ended after a second date with the lady of the month saying, "You're a really nice guy. I just don't feel the connection."

This morning, Phillip was optimistic about Julie, a woman he had met at a party, and was going to see for a second time the following evening.

Phillip and Julie had met the week before for coffee, and the plan for the following evening was to attend an art gallery opening, then go across the street to a trendy restaurant for a light dinner and drinks.

"How do you see it going?" I asked. "As you get toward the end of the dinner, how do you see your next steps, your conversation?"

"I'm an honest guy, you know. So I'll tell her I've had some dates online, but that I've put them all on hold, that I want to see where it goes with her."

"Really? You're going to tell her that?"

"Hey, I know women like to hear that," Phillip said. "Like last night, I replied to a woman online, and I told her that I had started seeing somebody, and that I don't think it's fair to date two women at a time."

"Seeing somebody? Were you referring to Julie?"

"Yeah. And the lady online told me she really thought that was good of me. She thought I was a really decent guy, and she admires me."

"But how's that helping you to get you a date with her, this lady online."

"Well," Phillip insisted, "she knows I'm a good guy."

"Whoa! First of all, you've got a long way to go before you can call this a committed relationship with Julie," I said. "If it doesn't work out with Julie, and you go back to this lady online, your chances with her are dead. Dead! How do you think she'll feel when you pop up saying, 'Hey, it didn't work out with the woman I started dating, this Julie, so how about we meet for a drink?' She's going to feel like second fiddle, and she's going to blow you off, man. She might make up something nice, but you're toast."

"But she's already said I'm a decent guy. She'll remember me for that. Most guys don't take that high road."

"Dude, I'm not saying be a bad boy, but there's an element of truth here to nice guys finishing last. You're not going steady with this Julie yet, so why even bring it up with your online friend? If you want to put her off, fine. If you want to meet her for a glass of wine, fine. You wouldn't be cheating on Julie. Until you're going steady with Julie or anybody, you're not cheating on her."

Phillip looked out the window.

So I continued. "Your chances with the lady online today are, at worst, dead, and at best, much lower than they were before you said that."

Phillip swallowed the pill bitterly, but indeed he swallowed it.

"Let's back up to Julie, though," I continued. "If you tell her that because of your second date, you won't see anyone else, you're going to scare her. You're going to give the impression that you're needy. You hardly know her, and you're telling her you've taken yourself out of the marketplace. If you don't scare her with apparent neediness, you're going to make her skeptical with disbelief. Either way, you're not going to get a third date. I'm all but certain."

"But I think she'll respect me for it."

"Dude, until you're going steady, you're not going steady! Don't put her needs before yours so early on. Be sensitive to her needs, but don't make her feel that you'll put your life on hold for her, at least not yet. Don't make her feel that you believe you're going steady!"

He began to see my point.

"Make *her* work a little bit, too. Let her see what a great guy you are and how much fun she could have if she hangs with you. Let her know you're in a good space, you're having fun and life is good. Why tell her more? If she asks about your dating status, smile, tell her you *are* dating."

I told him a bit about the *Pre-Selection* thing.

"Really. Make her work a little bit. Don't serve yourself up on a platter for her to pick and choose friend zone, casual dating, committed relationship or bruschetta with olives. You're the main course, man! You're not desperate. You're not easy. You're a catch. Make her put some fat bait on the line and cast it your way."

When the date with Julie started, Phillip wasn't sure if Julie appealed to him. He was attracted to her physically, and thought she was sweet, but she was a little reserved at first.

This gave Phillip just the courage he needed to play with confidence. At one point, he told Julie that he was indeed dating, but, sure, he'd like to have a committed relationship; that, for now, he was in a good space and just enjoying this phase.

Julie upped her game. She started giving him cues, flirting and giggling. Things warmed up. As Mr. Nice Guy Phillip walked Julie to her car, Julie couldn't find her car keys in her bottomless handbag. She made a joke about it and looked at him laughing.

Phillip took the cue and kissed her on the lips. Julie at first pulled back, looked him in the eye, then grabbed the back of his head and started making out with him.

After a few minutes, Julie whispered, "I should go."

"I should let you," Phillip said, "but I really don't want to."
"I don't want you to, either... but tonight, you're going to."

"Can I cook for you Saturday night?" Phillip asked. "My place?"

Julie said yes.

"Seven?"

Julie said yes, again.

She also said yes to pancakes Sunday morning.

The racing team never really said *no*. But they never really said *yes* to a steady, consulting relationship.

The team got a fast and easy deal – a quickie, of sorts – from the promotion agency, and the agency added more freebies after the one-nighter.

The agency hoped they were going steady. The Sr. VP not only shared this optimism with the team, but also with other contacts. Rumors about the agency-team hook up spread quickly through the marketplace.

This got back to the racing team faster than a lap on a one-mile oval. When they heard that the agency was working for them, they were surprised. They hadn't even discussed additional scope of work, let alone financial terms.

They weren't going steady. Their hearts hadn't yet been won. So the team went quiet.

Was the team they scared off? Did they think the agency was too easy? Desperate for love?

Internally, back at the agency, the hook up turned into one of several deals that drifted and drifted, and then never materialized.

Expectations were not met, and as Shakespeare wrote, expectation is the root of all heartache.

35

THE BEST PROPOSALS DON'T PROPOSE

It had been years since all the siblings had gotten together, and to celebrate that the two who lived farthest away were both in town at the same time, they threw a party on the Saturday night of a three-day weekend.

This prompted more friends and family to travel in. It turned into a bigger event than initially expected, so they took a terrace at a nearby hotel.

They rented a sound system, as some family members and friends were musicians. What an evening!

Much of the talk centered around a close cousin, Robert, and his girlfriend, Bettina. They had been seeing each other for about six months, and they were madly in love with each other.

Robert hadn't had a serious relationship since college, so most everyone's excitement was even bigger. And of course, Robert was over-the-moon happy, surrounded by these special friends, whom were all charmed by the lovely and glowing Bettina.

After dinner, a slow song played, and couples danced cheek-to-cheek. When it ended, Robert was onstage, with microphone in hand, as one of the singers said, "Hey, everybody! Robert's got a special announcement to make!"

Many expected Robert to announce that Bettina and he had gotten engaged. But Robert made it even more memorable.

After talking about two souls who had met in the park, he walked across the floor to Bettina. Some girls held their hands to their faces. Some guys were saying, "Can you believe this? He's going to *propose!*"

Robert was undaunted, as he stopped in front of the love of his life and said, "So, Bettina, I ask you. Will you marry me?"

Bettina blushed. She cried. And she said... "Yes!"

And that... was the beginning of the end.

The weekend ended and, of course, everyone made sure they congratulated Robert and Bettina. They asked all sorts of questions, many of which the couple couldn't answer.

Robert and Bettina returned to a normal week at their jobs, and Robert took Bettina to dinner the following Saturday.

And Bettina broke up with him.

Bettina knew that Robert wanted children soon, and she wanted to wait. Bettina wanted to finish her masters and settle into a job in finance. Bettina wanted so many things, and Robert wanted one thing... and he pushed forward with *his* proposal.

At the center of it were Bettina's emotions.

She was shocked, disappointed, *angered,* that Robert would propose to her, not just in such a spotlight moment in which it would be devastating to say, "No," or even, "Let's talk," but because they had not worked out so many things.

Bettina saw a handful of challenges that perhaps could have been over-come… but they had to be overcome before any proposal would be acceptable.

Now, it was too late. The deal was off.

In fact, it had never been a deal, in Bettina's mind. Not because she didn't love Robert, and not because she couldn't, with time, find a way to make it work, but because her trust had been broken when Robert simply jumped the gun. She didn't feel truly part of the process.

It's the same thing in a sale.

The best proposals don't propose. The best proposals confirm what's been discussed and agreed throughout a process of high engagement.

Not only is it unreasonable to make a proposal when all the business challenges have not been addressed, it's bad psychology.

Think of any business meeting when a challenge is being bantered about. If you have a great solution, perhaps even the *perfect* solution, and you shout it out in the first moment, it's almost never the solution that's taken.

In retrospect, do you think that if you would have let the moment flow a bit, asked some questions to go deeper into the challenge and offered your solution later, would it have stood a higher probability of being accepted?

This dynamic unfolds every day in relationships… and in sales.

Buyers need to be listened to. They need to go deep into the challenge itself. They need to feel like they're part of the solution.

If the solution comes off as your solitary, brilliant idea, and if it's proposed too early in the sales process, chances are that it won't be accepted.

Don't propose a solution too early. It's simply bad psychology. Very often, prospects will tell you they need a quick solution, like yesterday. Then, a week later, they tell you they're going to think about it or they're going to approach it a different way.

Involve the customer in building the solution. Engage them and win their hearts. It's human nature for people to be more committed to a solution that they have been a part of crafting.

Don't propose, period. That's right. Don't propose, even if it's guised as a proposal. Instead, do everything you can to discuss every aspect of your joint solution face-to-face.

The best proposals don't propose. They simply confirm what's been discussed and agreed.

Robert broke all the rules when proposing to Bettina. And Bettina broke up with him. Oh, what could've been.

There are still days,
I think of days I'd remove.
If I could go back,
With the power to pick and choose.

Oh, what could've been.
Oh, what wasn't.
Oh, what could've been.
What wasn't. What wasn't.
- 7 Worlds Collide, "What Could Have Been"

CHAPTER

36

↓

SEALED WITH A KISS

Closing a deal is easy if everything else in the sales process has been handled well and all concerns have been addressed.

I was once working with the sales team of a major London media firm. After securing the project, my first step was to assess critical issues and key objectives. I started with a face-to-face meeting with the CEO and CMO, who briefed me on the team's strength and weaknesses.

"Closers!" the CEO said.

"Yeah, we need closers!" the CMO agreed.

You could feel the testosterone in the room as both of these execs scratched their beards and deepened their voices.

These manly men wanted results, and that sales team had better put up the numbers.

"Closers!"

Isn't that the dream of every top manager, that their people close more deals?

The only problem with this is that you burn people out. You don't really help salespeople's long-term performance if you just say, "Close more business." They might respond successfully once or twice, but over the long-term, they begin to hear the kid crying wolf, and it's not a patient wolf.

After my CEO/CMO brief, I began meeting with their sales leaders as well as a cross-section of the salespeople and account execs. It quickly became obvious that the team knew how to close. This was the London media world, with lots of deadlines for program airings. These people knew how to ask for the deal.

The reason the team wasn't closing successfully was not their closing skills. The real reasons were two-fold.

One, they were doing other things earlier in the sales process without customer-focus, without love.

Two, pushing for the close was then simply making matters worse!

Pushy closer types kill trust.

The gap between what the alpha male CEO and CMO wanted versus where the team needed to improve was a chasm. I didn't mince my words when I told them. It was my duty to give them tough love.

"Your team doesn't need much work on their closing skills," I said. "We could spend a little time to review what works best when closing and what doesn't, but we won't be able to bring much in the way of new closing skills per se."

"So you can't help us get more business?" the CMO growled, his chin protruding like a cave man ready for battle. I don't know what testosterone smells like, but I could sense the temperature rising in the room.

"Oh, I can help you get more business," I said. "I can help your team sell more effectively. It's just that, when it comes to sales improvement and *which* skills to focus on, you won't see a bounce in your business if we provide you a workshop just in closing.

"The reason your team is not closing more business," I went on, "is that their skills in *other* areas of the sales process are where they're under-performing. They're not being consultative earlier in new prospect meetings, or even when bringing new opportunities to existing clients."

"But we need sales, and we need them fast," the CEO grumbled.

The CMO also made similar caveman sounds.

"If you want me to deliver a workshop on closing skills, with the expectation that you'll see a bump in your revenue the next month, I have to say, you're throwing your money away. Go ahead and look for other sales trainers, but if that's what they provide, I'll let *them* fail. I don't want your money as much as I want to effectively improve your team's performance."

I then gave them a skills gap analysis that charted where the team was under-performing. "If your team can improve in these areas, you will close more deals. But just focusing on closing, well, essentially, you'll be pushing your prospects through the dating process too quickly, too self-ishly, and then asking them to sleep with you. You gotta' show them some love and tenderness, boys. Really."

A few months earlier, I had, in fact, *closed* another client in London, only a few blocks away.

There was no testosterone in this close. It was so simple. I said *nothing.*

The *client* closed the deal. (Not only did she feel she was in control at the conclusion of the deal, she also continued trusting me through the solution-delivery stage *and* more work flowed my way.)

It was our second face-to-face meeting. I had sent her the materials for this meeting two days earlier. Now we sat in her office and made subtle tweaks to my materials. The buyer signals were all *go*. Her body language was positive. Her head was nodding.

So I said… nothing.

There wasn't anything more I could say, lest I'd be going backwards in the sales process.

I admit, I was *tempted* to say something, but silence was the right move… at least… for… a few… more… seconds.

"Jack, let's move ahead with this," she said. "If you can tweak the scope and deliverables section as we just discussed and attach it to a vendor form that I'll send you, it will be nothing but a formality. Let's go ahead for September."

The buyer wanted to move forward. Any overt *closing* line would simply not be showing the love. Because I let her close herself, she felt as though she was in control, not pushed. Her trust level was high, and she acted with confidence.

If this were a date, she would've stared at my lips, and we would have kissed.

A first kiss is indisputably the pinnacle of the dating process.

Nearly every romantic relationship takes on a new dimension once the first kiss happens. And by kiss, let's be clear, not a peck on the cheek kiss, but a juicy one on the lips.

A first kiss does not mean marriage is going to happen. It doesn't mean sex will happen. But a kiss is a major step that two people dating must get to in order for the relationship to be defined as romantic.

The first kiss is a major step that brings clear focus to the future of the relationship, to both lovers' expectations and intentions. In business terms, a juicy kiss is clearly a *Letter Of Intent*.

This is the last time I'll mention *Hitch, The Love Doctor*.

In one scene, Hitch is talking with Albert who had, shall we say, underperformed the night before. No, he had not under-performed in the bedroom; he was a long way from the promised land, in fact. Albert had under-performed in advancing a casual date with Allegra toward a romantic relationship.

Albert told Hitch that, as the date ended, he asked Allegra if he could kiss her.

"You don't ask a woman if you can if you can kiss her," Hitch shrieked. *"JUST KISS HER!"*

Albert was still questioning how to make such a move.

So Hitch explained that Albert should move ninety percent of the way toward Allegra's lips, and that he should let her move in the other ten per cent.

Indeed, the woman needs to feel she has some control in the first kiss.

As do customers in the final agreement. Sometimes all you have to do is bring them 90 per cent of the way, and they'll take the initiative to move forward the last ten per cent.

I've actually been kissed after closing a business deal... but not on the lips.

↓

TOUGH LOVE & HAPPILY EVER AFTER

So you've seduced, engaged and won the heart of your customer, and you both know that relationships are more fruitful and productive if they are long-term.

Relationships rarely work if expectations are not managed early on.

So once you and your love-interest customer have determined that you both want a committed relationship, it's still probably too early to move in together. It's time to negotiate.

No, it's *not* the time to get everything you can. It's *not* the time to throw that love away.

Focus on getting what you need, indeed, but also help your lover get what he or she needs.

There's no better time for *tough love* than when you negotiate.

Neither of these two words, *tough* or *love*, should take priority over the other. You can be tough in a kind way. It's called firmness.

You can be loving in a responsible way. It's called fairness.

So that's the mindset and the heart-set. What's the approach?

There's an old adage: "If a deal seems too good to be true, it probably is."

How some parties negotiate a great deal for themselves while bringing their future partner to their knees moving forward is simply mind-boggling. Even more mind-boggling is that it happens every day.

Do you want to have a partner who is squeezed to the point of not breathing, as you move forward in implementing your relationship?

Yikes! How long do you think your great deal will last?

Be aware of the fallout from a failed partnership.

Be aware of the emotional baggage and material damage that a divorce brings to *both* parties. Break-ups have huge downsides.

So do failed joint ventures and business relationships. Not only are they costly, but they can also kill the trust other stakeholders may have in you. The marketplace keeps no secrets.

As Leigh L. Thompson wrote in *The Truth About Negotiations*, the best negotiators do not focus on *the deal*. They focus on the future business, *the relationship*, after the deal is done.

Negotiate a deal that's good for you, indeed. If you use tough love by being transparent as to why you need certain things, the other party will more likely negotiate with transparency, too. The other party will more likely work toward a business relationship that enhances your chances of success, in addition to theirs.

I once had the privilege of sitting across the negotiating table from Patricia Straker, although at times it didn't feel like a privilege.

Patricia knew the art of tough love. She was one of the top sponsorship professionals in Canada.

My team and I had sold her firm, Royal Bank of Canada, the sponsorship rights to the 1999 Pan American Games, to be hosted by Winnipeg.

In our first meeting with Royal Bank, Patricia bought into our vision of the best Pan Am Games of the century… and the high sponsorship price tag that came with it.

She also saw the tremendous value in the sponsorship.

Clearly, we wanted Royal Bank's sponsorship for the money, but also for the name and for the partnership. Adding Royal Bank to our sponsor group would give us *street cred* around Toronto and around Canada.

Patricia was tough, but fair.

Our only response was to be firm, but fair.

The negotiations were long and sometimes tense, but they were always civil. They were always focused on the future partnership, not on the deal.

Royal Bank needed to secure certain conditions. Yet they never tried to reduce our price tag, and they always demonstrated they would do every-thing reasonable in their power to help us make these the best Pan Am Games of the century.

All too often, once a deal is done, one or both parties go away calculating how they can extract the most for themselves moving forward.

Ouch! Not a lot of love there, is there? And probably not a good business relationship in place after the negotiation, either.

When the dust settled on our negotiation, however, Patricia executed her part of the deal and, as mentioned, she and Royal Bank helped us make the Games great. She was one of the best business partners I ever worked with in my 12 years in sports sponsorship.

As the Games approached, I realized I loved her. Professionally, of course, I absolutely loved Patricia.

We had a solid friendship, but the foundation was respect for each other's professionalism (at least that's what I felt toward her).

We would talk business and we would talk life. Sometimes we laughed so hard that tears would roll down our eyes. The paradox of the tough love negotiations was that the relationship moving forward was trusting and relaxed.

We each felt accountable to the other, and we knew it was mutual.

After the negotiation and as the Games approached, we even hit some unexpected bumps in the road. We had left some stones unturned in the negotiation.

As is typical to events of this nature, there were areas that neither of us had foreseen until Games operations started to be implemented. We had to go back to the negotiation table. The tone was business-like, but it was never as tough as the first negotiation, when we had moved from pitch to contract.

The relationship worked. We had won each others' hearts.

Patricia said some of the nicest things about me out in the sponsorship marketplace. While compliments are nice, they're even nicer when they come from someone who has a rock solid reputation.

Patricia was known to be tough, but never unfair.

Tough love is responsible love. Tough love is responsible negotiation.

Tough love is good business.

CHAPTER 38

YOUR LOVER IS NOT ALWAYS RIGHT. NOR IS YOUR CUSTOMER.

One of the biggest false truths in business is the old maxim, "The customer is always right."

Do you really believe, deep down inside, that your customers are always right?

Of course you don't. So why would you let them believe it?

If you love yourself first, and thereby enable yourself to do what's best for your customer, then why lie to them?

To let the customer believe they're right when you don't believe it is a lie.

You're lying to yourself, and you're lying to your customer.

To say your lover is always right is like saying, "I'll do anything for sex, for a relationship, for approval."

To say the customer is always right is like saying, "I'll do anything for your money."

It might earn you points in the short-term but, over the long haul, this will only dig you deeper into a toxic relationship. Toxic relationships are not good for your karma. They're not good for your reputation. They're not good for your bottom line.

Your best customers want – and deserve – your brutal honesty. So does your worthy romantic partner!

Be confident, and know what you stand for. By loving yourself, you'll be able to give your best love to your customers. If you truly love your customers, you'll do what you know and feel is best for them. Telling them they're wrong should be done in the same way as in a healthy romantic partnership.

Frame it in the positive, in a tone of what's *right* for them.

Be clear in outlining the consequences of taking the wrong decision or action, and in outlining the benefits of taking the right action.

Of course, you will meet some resistance. Listen proactively. Understand their concerns and empathize with them.

Then handle as you would any objection… with tender, loving care.

"SORRY" SEEMS TO BE THE HARDEST WORD

It was so early in my career that the fax machine was still the business medium of choice.

We had pitched a potential partner on an exciting marketing platform, and they liked it. We were now negotiating deliverables and returns.

A cantankerous lawyer on the other side of the table fired a shot at our team. "You folks were supposed to fax us the payment schedule. We never received it!"

Their Head of Marketing tossed in another shot. "We're flying in the dark here!"

A thousand negative impulses went through my body and mind in a split-second. I had drafted the fax for my boss, but due to travel schedules, a stressed-out personal assistant and plain ol' high work loads, it never got sent.

Would this turn into finger pointing? Would this slow us down?

In the next split second, however, my boss reversed all the bad karma. He shrugged his shoulders and said, "Sorry. That was my fault. I saw it on my desk but didn't act on it. Let me call the office right now and see if my assistant can dig it out."

You could almost hear the pressure in the room drop like the hiss a deflating tire.

My young head was telling me to shut up, play it safe and let the tire deflate, but my gut told me otherwise. So I leaned forward.

"I have it," I said. "Sorry, I should have followed up to see if it got sent."

My boss smiled and said, "No, no. You left it with me and I dropped the ball. Shit happens."

There were chuckles around the room as everyone focused on the payment schedule that I was passing out. The finger pointing quickly went by the wayside.

The future is more important than the past.

It wasn't about the payment schedule, really. It was about everyone moving forward, not staying stuck in the proverbial shit that had happened.

If we hadn't apologized, if we would have made up some stupid excuse, the shit would most likely have risen above everybody's knees and soon covered the meeting room table. The pressure would have risen in the room and we would have gotten sidetracked.

Our prospect would have been looking at us as though we were either incompetent, unreliable or both. Instead we seemingly formed a bond with them. We were confident enough in ourselves to understand that we're all imperfectly human, and little shit happens every day. Onward and upward.

Easy, right?

Indeed, to some.

But to many, *Sorry* seems to be the hardest word, thank you, Elton John.

Sorry shouldn't be the hardest word. It should be one of the easiest words, because as vulnerable as you may feel, you actually win hearts when you use *Sorry* genuinely.

Sorry doesn't mean, "I'm wrong, you're right." It doesn't mean, "I should be penalized, you should win the point."

If you're stuck in that mindset, then you'll apologize too infrequently, especially in business and especially in front of prospective customers.

You can tailor *Sorry* to mean what you want it to mean, because the spirit and tone in which you say it counts, too.

In tone, it could go like this. "Oops. Too bad this has happened. I'm big enough to admit I had a role in it. I'm great enough to focus on accomplishing something big here. Sorry about that. Let's move on."

Gaining a little competitive advantage doesn't hurt, either.

As Craig Dowden wrote in *Psychology Today* in 2014, *The Three Keys To A Real Apology*, "Despite our history with conflict, the vast majority of us struggle with making amends. We either avoid the conversation or make things worse with an awkward 'non-apology.'"

Dowden further writes that the positive outcomes of apologizing, in both personal and business relationships, are two-fold.

"First, the transgressor was seen as more valuable as a relationship partner, since the apology signified the level of importance the transgressor placed on the relationship. The apology also made the individual who was harmed feel more confident in the strength and stability of the relationship moving forward.

"Second, and equally important, the transgressor was seen as less likely to engage in hurtful behaviors in the future and genuinely desiring that the conflict end."

And that's why we should take the lead in apologizing. It puts you in a stronger position.

When you deflect, deny or avoid a problem, tension usually rises. Defenses go up. Bonds are broken. Trust is lost, and if you're the seller – or a romantic partner – you're the loser.

When you apologize, tension usually drops. Defenses go down. Bonds are built. Trust is gained… and you're a winner.

Romantic and personal relationships are endangered when pride gets in the way, and one of the most common behaviors associated with pride is refusing to apologize.

It's easy to protect one's ego by refusing to apologize, but that only hurts the relationship.

Apologize quickly, and others not only let you off the hook, they often give you the benefit of the next doubt.

The sooner you apologize, the easier it is to do so. It's that simple.

Think of any situation in your professional, romantic or personal life when it really was incumbent upon you to apologize, but you delayed. Wouldn't it have been easier to do so shortly after the incident, or even immediately?

Doesn't it get more difficult as time passes?

All that negative energy is a drain on your karma and damaging to your relationship.

The sooner you say, "Oops, sorry," the less collateral damage is done. Not only will you move on sooner, you will leave less wreckage in your wake. You'll have good karma, and you'll win more hearts.

Go easy on yourself. Be secure in your imperfections.

Sure, customers want to deal with competent people, but, like romantic partners, they also want to deal with secure people.

Spiritual leaders throughout the ages have gone deep into the concept of forgiveness. Perhaps Mahatma Gandhi said it best. "The weak can never forgive. Forgiveness is the attribute of the strong."

Sorry is the embodiment of forgiveness, of self-forgiveness, of strength, of winning hearts.

If you never admit to even the smallest mistakes, the other party will admit them for you.

If you apologize quickly and genuinely and move on, the other party will admire you, trust you and love you more. You'll experience less pain in your sales cycle, and probably more *sales*, to boot.

If you don't believe me, well, I'm happy to leave it and move on, sorry.

Now where were we, darling?

40

OXYTOCIN, DOPAMINE & THE TWO-YEAR ITCH

No matter how socially conditioned we are, there is one force of nature that will continue to drive any romantic relationship. Biochemistry.

Religion and legal systems are valiant attempts to keep us civil but, as outlined earlier, caveman genetics are at the center of our biological operating systems. Neanderthal behavior is still within each and every one of us to some degree.

Throw in the industrial revolution, the digital revolution, dual career paths and birth control, and modern humanity has evolved from the *Flintstones* to the *Jetsons*. Our biochemistry, however, has only evolved from *Flintstones* to *Flintstones 2.0*.

Romantic love is a beautiful thing, but it's also a biological thing. It drives the survival of the species, which requires the survival of the offspring, which, in turn, shapes the behavior of the mates.

When we fall in love today, the forces of primal biochemistry are still at play. The flow of hormones waxes and wanes, driving behavioral patterns, from falling in love right through to breaking up!

When we first fall in love, oxytocin and dopamine are released into the blood. These two hormones put the *crazy* in crazy love.

Indeed, newfound love changes our behavior. It makes us throw caution to the wind. It can cause us to move to a new city, or even a new continent, to be with that special soul mate. Any risk seems surmountable.

"Forget the finances, we'll make this work."

So while this sounds like modern life, it's actually as old as humankind itself. Go back a few thousand years, and it was more like this.

A male and a female fell in love. Few, if any, forces could keep them apart.

Parents may have objected. Community elders may have tried to keep them apart. But the lovers persisted.

Together, they would be one.

Within a few months, pregnancy was inevitable.

Nine months after that, the baby arrived – a fragile and vulnerable infant. The mother was also vulnerable because she had given most of her energy to gestating this tiny creature, and now she was nurturing and protecting it.

The father was pitching in at the home front. He was doing the heavy lifting while continuing the daily hunting.

The couple was still in love but now focused on making all the home economics work – the survival of the offspring, the survival of the family and, by default, the survival of the species.

What's really behind all this is biochemistry and a surge of oxytocin and dopamine in the blood. These two hormones drive love and romantic commitment… at least in the early stages.

Survival of the species is also what's behind the waning of these love hormones after approximately two sets of winter, spring, summer and fall. After about two years, romantic love fades… unless we are committed at a higher level than just grunting into the cave's love nest and keeping the offspring healthy and safe.

Today, humans are more enlightened, or so we like to believe. Perhaps this is why the average marrying age continues to get older. Perhaps this is why we only move in together. Perhaps this is why we wait to *develop our careers* before having children.

Perhaps this is why Irish grandmothers tell their granddaughters, "Don't marry him until the second winter passes."

These wise women have seen these human behavioral patterns in action over generations. (Or maybe they've studied biochemistry.)

Oh, dear! We've jumped ahead tens of thousands of years. Back to the cave.

The vulnerable infant became a toddler. Now that the toddler no longer depended fully on the mother for every essence of survival, the mother could also focus on a few other things.

And so could the father.

While the mother's interest in romance and sex with her partner still existed, it was nothing like it was two years earlier. The same went for the father, who started hunting again for bigger sloths, farther from the home fire, where perhaps he stumbled upon another fertile woman.

Oh, the two-year itch!

With home life less exciting, this new, fertile woman looked sooooo gooooood!

And the oxytocin-dopamine cycle started all over again.

Meanwhile, back at the home front, the mother hadn't taken her head out of the proverbial nest, so prospecting for suitors was not a central part of her mindset. Of course, she certainly felt that her mate wasn't around the home fire as much as he used to be. Perhaps her first offspring would be her last mating… or perhaps another suitable mate, in search of the next big kill, came along and happened upon this fertile cavewoman who also looked sooooo goooood!

Gimme' some of that oxytocin, baby! Gimme' some dopamine!

Fast forward again to the 21st century. The oxytocin and dopamine cycle impacts women just as strongly as it impacts men, not because the human biochemistry has changed one bit, but because we now have additional facilitators that drive our romantic wanderlust: birth control, dual careers and Facebook.

The two-year itch is a reality.

No one's guilty. Everyone's surviving.

So to keep the relationship together, the real work often starts at around the two-year mark. Biochemistry hasn't changed, only the environment has. Social conditioning and home economics aren't what they used to be, and wanderlust is inevitable.

The two-year itch is a biological reality in mating.

Is the two-year itch a reality in business, as well?

We've heard of *honeymoon periods* for new CEOs and new managers. Likewise, employees often begin wondering after a couple of years if their employers are as fantastic as they first thought during their first month on the job.

Is it any different between vendors and clients, salespeople and customers?

In the advertising and communications business, agency reviews often come up after two or three years.

Is this because the agencies' creative solutions are less effective after two years, or because the agency leaders aren't, um, good in bed anymore, or because the clients are simply getting a little wanderlust and a little bit of that two-year itch?

Could it be that the client's oxytocin and dopamine are on the wane?

Have a look at your industry. Have a look at your clients!

Being good in bed isn't enough to keep the home fire burning.

Delivering textbook customer service is no longer enough to keep a client's business.

How's your relationship after the honeymoon period?

Will it survive the wane of oxytocin from your customer's biochemistry?

Are you working on it before the dopamine fades, before the review period? Are you continuing to win their hearts?

Or are you out hunting for bigger sloths?

41

IN A NEW YORK MINUTE

Lying here in the darkness,
I hear the sirens wail.
Somebody's going to emergency,
Somebody's going to jail.
If you find someone to love in this world,
You better hang on tooth and nail.
The wolf is always at the door.

In a New York Minute,
Everything can change.
In a New York minute,
Things can get a little strange.
In a New York minute,
Everything can change,
In a New York Minute.

And in these days,
When darkness falls early,
And people rush home
To the ones they love,
You better take a fool's advice,
And take care of your own.
One day they're here,
And the next day they're gone.

In a New York Minute,
Everything can change,
In a New York Minute.

The above lyrics from The Eagles are wise words that lovers – and sales-people – often don't heed until it's too late.

Don't wait until it's too late.

With few exceptions, the best customer is the one you have. The energy, resources and hard costs of securing new customers are always higher than maintaining existing customers and keeping them happy.

Of course we should seek and secure new business, as that's the key to growth. But one step forward and one step back is no way to run a business or earn commissions. Losing good customers can be demotivating to yourself as a salesperson, and devastating to the health of your organization as a leader.

Sometimes the tea leaves that need to be read aren't even tea leaves. They're not smoke signals. They're often clearly stated words.

"Honey, I'm unhappy. We seem to do everything for the kids. What about the two of us?"

Why is this so often met with indifference? All too often, partners look back at their indifference after a break-up and know they could've done better.

Winning hearts is great. Great! But keeping hearts is even greater.

Much like lovers send signals and prospects send signals, so do existing customers. Listening is critical in love, in a sale and in customer service.

Just as critical is taking action on what you hear. Because in a New York Minute, everything can change.

Busy couples often get caught in ruts. That's one of the values of baby-sitters, date nights and romantic weekends.

Why not take your existing customers out for dates? The occasional working lunch is probably not enough. Do something different with your customers, one-on-one, and then find the right moment to explore the good, the bad and the ugly.

"How can I make you happy, dear?"

Hold on to your customers… tooth and nail.

It's the new golden rule.

Love unto others as you would have them love unto you.

42

LOVE CONQUERS ALL

"Love is the bridge between you and everything."
- Rumi

The best salespeople in any industry are *loved* by their customers.

How do they do it?

They start with self-love. They have confidence. They believe in themselves.

The love their products so much that they are passionate about bringing such opportunities to their customers.

They are not seen as takers, but as givers.

They don't push customers through their own sales cycle. They pull customers through their purchasing cycle.

They keep it simple in marketing, and then they go deeper in sales.

They seduce new prospects with simplicity, with compelling messages that spark emotions as much as they catalyze rational thoughts, and they build attraction by sparking curiosity, by teasing.

The best salespeople don't talk too much about themselves, though. They engage customers by shifting the conversation away from themselves and toward their customers as early as they can.

They ask great questions and listen actively.

They win customers' hearts by building solutions together and handling objections in a spirit of bonding, by winning the point while enhancing the relationship.

They earn commitment by letting the customers feel they're in control, even though, as wooing lovers, the salesperson assumes the responsibility for moving the relationship forward.

They know that business is about relationships, during the sale and after the sale. They hold on to their good customers and don't assume that repeat business will just happen through good implementation. They keep the love alive.

Essentially, the best salespeople win hearts by spreading the love.

In sales as it is in romance, it's all about honest communication, deep understanding and mutual trust.

Remember the first chapter of this book, *When Sally Met Harry?*

Harry did everything right at the networking event when Sally walked in.

He did everything right at their first date, um, first appointment, at the wine bar.

And he did everything right when Sally introduced him to her management team.

Harry sold Sally a very big solution, and her company became one of his biggest customers in his business start-up.

Harry also found the love of his life this way. He had been dating, but didn't commit until he found a partner who suited him, and to whom he suited.

Harry is a true character with a true story, like every character in this book, most of whose names I've changed for obvious reasons.

Harry knows the universal truth: the more you give, the more you get... in romance... and in sales... and in all human relationships.

Poets write about it.

Songwriters sing about it.

Artists of every genre endeavor to express it.

This is the human condition.

Love conquers all.

ABOUT THE AUTHOR
JACK VINCENT

Jack is a sales advisor, speaker and trainer who divides his time between Luzern, Switzerland and Woodstock, NY.

His first love was writing. Then he hit puberty. "It's a good thing I fell in love with writing first," Jack laughs, "because I probably would have been too distracted to put pen to paper."

That near obsession with the essence of human nature was seen as a handicap by some of Jack's high school teachers, but it was seen as a strength by his most memorable journalism professor at Syracuse University's S.I. Newhouse School of Public Communications. In Jack's last semester of his senior year, MAG 505's Professor Keats said, "I don't care if you write fact or fiction in this course. What I want is the truth! I want you to write about the timeless and universal condition of human nature."

"I'm an over-communicator to the point of no return," Jack says. "I really see it as a flaw. I can't help myself. At the same time, the human condition is where wisdom lies, even in business. I see Shakespeare in the meeting room. I see Rumi in great presentations. To my pleasant surprise, I've been called a *poet in a business suit.* The only thing that's changed since then is... I've lost the suit."

After a year as a news and feature writer at his hometown newspaper, love brought him to Barcelona, Spain where, as it turned out, English-language journalists weren't in high demand. Fortunately, the world of international marketing communications had a place for an over-communicator, so Jack found himself selling and marketing wine, then fast-moving consumer goods, and then high-profile sports events.

He's marketed and sold the global sponsorships and TV rights to some of the world's most exciting sports properties, including the Olympic Games, World Cup Football/Soccer and the ATP Men's Tennis Tour.

He's sold to – and provided sales training, presentation skills and leadership development to – some of the world's leading companies. An abbreviated list includes Coca-Cola, MasterCard, Visa, Boston Consulting Group, IBM, ESPN, NBC Universal, Eurovision/EBU, Who Wants To Be A Millionaire?, Phonak, Emerson and Panasonic, as well as numerous startups and independent consultants.

As guest lecturer at Lucerne University of Applied Sciences & Arts, Jack uses non-traditional approaches to hold the attention of students. "I'm the disruptive one," he insists.

He has facilitated strategic retreats for corporations in far-off places and has led panels for Non-Governmental Organizations in Davos during the World Economic Forum. He's frequently asked to moderate corporate events and industry conferences alike, such as *Enterprise Marketing 2.0* in Amsterdam and *InnoCos Beauty* in New York.

The host of TEDxLuzern and TEDxZug, Jack is a TEDx speaker himself. His 2014 TEDxLugano Talk, *A Sale Is A Love Affair*, was overwhelmingly voted the best talk of the day by the audience.

Jack is also a Distinguished Toastmaster and the 2006 European Champion of the Toastmasters Humorous Speech Contest, with his memorable speech, *The Love Coach*. If over-communicating about his obsession isn't enough, he also officiates weddings and writes love poetry.

You can follow Jack's blog at jackvincent.com. You can also find him on Twitter @JackVincent.

WHO'S SPREADING THE LOVE

"Jack leaves you breathless…"

This book is every bit as fun to read as it is important for the success of your business. Smart, passionate, driven, Jack leaves you breathless with this one.
> — CHRIS BROGAN, CEO OWNER MEDIA GROUP

"A sales professional… and a romantic at heart."

Jack is a very talented sales and business professional, as well as a romantic at heart. Both aspects shine through in this finely written and insightful book.
> — JAMIE GRAHAM, CEO TEAM MARKETING,
> MARKETERS OF UEFA CHAMPIONS LEAGUE

"Will help you gain new confidence in growing your business…"

As a small business owner with a fairly high record of closing new business, I read Jack Vincent's A Sales Is a Love Affair *with a bit of cynicism. After all, I already know it all, right? Wrong!*

The more I read, the more my heart began to sink. Yes, the "chase" does sound familiar. Yes, I often leave meetings without the prospect having any skin in the game. Yes, I often hear excuses as to why someone isn't making a decision or, worse, never hear from them again.

This book will tear you down, build you back up, and help you gain new confidence in growing your business.

> — GINI DIETRICH, FOUNDER & CEO
> ARMENT DIETRICH, AUTHOR OF SPIN SUCKS

"A mashup between sales training and relationship counseling…"

Fun to read and really worth the journey for anyone trying to understand how to sell better (and love stronger).

Jack leads us through a mashup between front-line executive sales training and relationship counseling to reinforce that building trust, earning respect, listening and partnering are the traits we can't forget if we want success.

And, when you're done reading it for business, pass it on to your spouse or partner.

— John Kristick, Global CEO, GroupM ESP

"Inspires the mind, touches the heart and lifts the spirit..."

A Sale Is A Love Affair *energized me from the moment I picked it up and scanned the Table of Contents.*

Selling is about creating emotional bonds. People want to be respected and loved. Jacks' stories encourage you to do this by being natural, honest and real.

When I met my wife, we energized each other. At zai, we built a team that was energized by our mission to design skis with a soul. Working hard means doing everything with loving energy. And now I read this book and I can envision how we can effectively share this deep emotion with our customers and drive our business.

A Sale Is A Love Affair *inspires the mind, touches the heart and lifts the spirit.*

— Benedikt Germanier, CEO *zai*

"Experiences in the boardroom, barroom and bedroom…"

*For Jack Vincent, love and sales are two human activities that go hand-in-hand.
In* A Sale is a Love Affair, *he explores the similarities between the two, and
explains how and why sales people should treat their clients the way a person should
treat his or her romantic partner.*

*Drawing on his own, and others', experiences in the boardroom, barroom and
bedroom, Jack works with the painstaking care of a microbiologist to code the two
strands of the sales-love double helix. The result is this book and its 42 punchy and
entertaining chapters.*

Whether you're looking to make a sale or win the heart of the love of your life,
A Sale is a Love Affair *contains a variety of insights to help you seal the deal.*

— JOHN ZIMMER, BARRISTER & SOLICITOR,
PROFESSIONAL SPEAKER AND TRAINER,
MANNEROFSPEAKING

"Great humor, colorful language… emotional connection."

*The parallel between love and sales is entertaining and insightful: this is an
impressive collection of real life examples connecting love (attraction, sex, romantic
relationships) with sales (interest, making the deal, customer relationships).*

*The author's great humor and colorful language depict the situations vividly.
Jack gives clear advice on how to apply this experience to become a better sales person
through greater emotional connection.*

— FRODE HVARING, HEAD OF HUMAN
RESOURCES, EBU/EUROVISION

"Not just about influencing minds, but also about winning hearts…"

A Sale Is A Love Affair *is edgy, almost outrageous and beyond beautiful. That's what makes it so profound and so human.*

Jack smacks you in the head in a raw way and touches your heart in a spiritual way. He shows us how to honor ourselves first, which enables us to deeply connect with customers and drive more sales.

The book is loaded with anecdotes and stories that are charged with emotion and energy.

As a dating and love coach, it's clear to me that he also shows us how to connect more deeply in our romantic relationships… and that love and sales are not just about influencing minds, but also about winning hearts.

— SUZANNE MULLER-HEINZ, AUTHOR OF
Loveable – 21 Practices for Being in
a Loving & Fulfilling Relationship.

"Irreverent… fun and simple…"

Irreverent and straightforward. In a fun and simple way, Jack uses the analogy of romantic relationships to effectively explain the intricacies of great salesmanship.

Whether you are looking to expand your client base or find the love of your life, this book will help you improve your game and increase your chances at both.

— SEBASTIÁN LORA, SPEAKER & TRAINER,
DECLAMATORIA

"An epiphany for many sales professionals."

An outstanding love story, this book is a revolution. It should have been written a long time ago, and now we have it!

Jack did not create a non-fiction book. Nor did he write a fiction book. Instead, he created a unique reading experience that unifies a tough business challenge (sales) with a soft and purely emotional topic (love).

Jack is not the first to point out the importance of emotions for successful sales. But he is the first one who does it with such humour, passion and conviction that I could not help to suck in the entire book and to immediately imagine my own sales challenges being like a love affair.

A Sale Is A Love Affair, carefully read and applied, will be an epiphany for many sales professionals. But it doesn't stop there. The best part is that this book sticks with the reader. It is the antithesis of any book about "sales methods." Instead, it transmits stories to the reader that everyone can connect with: love stories. Consequently, it has the power to transform entire sales teams and dramatically increases sales success.

I highly recommend this book to all people in any sales situation, as well as to any business leader of any type of organisation. Because of its entertaining style, it is also a perfect gift for colleagues and business partners.

Definitely one of the must-reads of 2015!

— Volkmar Völzke, CEO,
New Pace Consulting

"Charmingly unapologetic..."

It's easy to love Jack. He knows what he's talking about, he does it in a charmingly unapologetic way and he's not afraid to share all his vast sex-related experiences that, I suspect in this book, he's disguising as those of his many friends... or ex-friends, once they read this!

On top of that, Jack has decades of experience and insight in the profession of selling. So while there are great sales tools in this book, the link with the many adventures into the world of love, romance and, yes, sex, make these tools more memorable and deployable.

A Sale Is A Love Affair *kept me reading and wanting more. It made me want to go right out and test these new skills... in the field of sales, that is.*

— JERZY ZIENTKOWSKI, FOUNDER, SPEAKERSLAIR

"A new approach to customer-focused selling..."

Jack makes insightful links that build the case for salespeople to engage their clients as romantic partners. A Sale Is A Love Affair *will lead to a new approach in customer-focused selling.*

—STEFAN AMMANN, BUSINESS COLLEAGUE